"Cynthia Ruchti has created a beautifully written, practical guide offering help, hope, and a dash of humor. It is possible to help your aging parents as their health and minds fail without losing yours! We are right in the middle of this season and Cynthia's biblical and practical wisdom is like a big glass of iced tea on a hot and humid summer's day."

—**Pam and Bill Farrel**, authors of forty-five books, including the bestselling *Men Are Like Waffles, Women Are Like Spaghetti*

"I love this book and wish it had been available when I cared for my own mom the last three years of her life. The chapters are short but packed full of great suggestions with perfect bite sized wisdom to help you navigate the rough waters. Cynthia's beautiful poems and prayers will comfort your weary soul as you love and care for your own aging parent."

—**Carole Lewis**, director emeritus, First Place 4 Health, author of *Live Life, Right Here, Right Now*

"Much truth and wisdom are packed into this easy-to-read volume. I laughed and cried as I read it, recalling memories of caring for my parents and thinking: I wish I'd had a book this helpful to read! The author is vulnerable and transparent, which makes *As My Parents Age* such an essential—even delightful—resource for caretakers."

—**Carolyn Curtis**, speaker and author of *Women and C. S. Lewis*

"With sensitivity, grace, and compassion Cynthia Ruchti eloquently addresses the many and varied realities of life with an aging parent. She helps us truly honor our mother and father while being fully honest about the struggles and her dependence on God for strength, discernment, and perspective. *As My Parents Age* is an invaluable resource for anyone navigating life with an aging parent."

—**Laura Taggert,** licensed marriage and family therapist, author of *Making Love Last*

"Because of the discoveries of science and medicine, we live in an age when many of us will find ourselves caregivers for our parents. Cynthia Ruchti has prepared us well in this book. She offers forty reflections dealing with matters we will need answers to as our roles reverse and we become the parents and our parents become the children."

—**Susan Osborn**, author of over thirty books

"I want my kids to read this book. And I'll bet my ninety-five-year-old mom is glad I read it. Written with hope and kindness, this is practical truth-talking from someone who has walked this road."

—**Betsy A. Barber**, PsyD, Associate Director,
Institute for Spiritual Formation, Talbot School of Theology

"Having recently experienced the emotional crisis and physical infirmities of caring for an aging parent with my precious father-in-law, I hold deep appreciation for Cynthia Ruchti's touching, poignant, and helpful book, *As My Parents Age*. Unafraid to reach into our raw places, Cynthia holds our hands while we travel a difficult road, and through her grace-filled words, we not only find comfort, but strength to carry on."

—**Anita Agers Brooks**, international speaker, inspirational life coach,
and award-winning author of *Getting Through What You Can't Get Over*

"I wish I would have had *As My Parents Age* available to me when I cared for my mother and my mother-in-law. I think Cynthia Ruchti's wisdom, encouragement, and empathy would have empowered me to care for them with greater tenderness and understanding. Her short inspirational chapters, practical ideas, personal stories, and biblical wisdom can be quickly read by busy caregivers. I'm so glad this book is now available."

—**Kathy Collard Miller**, international speaker and author of many books
including *Pure Hearted: The Blessings of Living Out God's Glory*

"A beautiful, gentle, insightful, and sensitive book for anyone with an aging parent, guardian, or friend. Escape regret and embrace the final season of your loved one's life with Cynthia's warm and wise words and stories . . . because you don't get a second chance."

—**Jane Rubietta**, international speaker and author of nineteen books, including *Heartbeat of a Mother* and *Worry Less So You Can Live More*

"Cynthia Ruchti has given us a gift. With tenderness and grace she takes a delicate subject and turns caring for our aging parents from burden to beautiful. Her words and process impart courage and practical help to walk through this stage of life."

—**Debbie Alsdorf**, speaker, author of *Deeper* and *The Faith Dare*, founder of Design4Living Ministries

"Cynthia Ruchti, how did you know *As My Parents Age* would be just the resource I needed? Because you have covered forty different situations, I was able to find exactly what applied to my life today, knowing this compassionate resource would also serve me well in the future. I intend to purchase a copy of this book for each of our sons so they are equipped when we become the 'aging parents' and they become the 'custodial children.'"

—**Kendra Smiley**, conference speaker, author of *Journey of a Strong-Willed Child, Live Free,* and *Mother of the Year: 365 Days of Encouragement for Devoted Moms*

"I cared for my mom in her last years. Those days would have been easier, less stressful, and more meaningful if I'd read *As My Parents Age* first. The stories of people who have also lived in the sandwich between being a child and parenting your parents will prove that you aren't alone. Cynthia Ruchti's wonderful, poetic, life-giving words will help you through this difficult time of your life. Read it and read it again!"

—**Karen Porter**, speaker, coach, and author of *Speak Like Jesus*

"In *As My Parents Age*, Cynthia Ruchti reshapes minds and attitudes as she prompts us to see obligations as opportunities. I regret this book was not available when my father was dying with cancer, but I am so grateful I have its wisdom to guide me through my mother's walk with Alzheimer's. *As My Parents Age* will help you focus, rejoice, understand, and celebrate the lives of loved ones while you still have them. This is one of the best and most timely books I've read in many years."

—**Ace Collins**, Christy award-winning author

"Surely Cynthia Ruchti has been reading my journal! *As My Parents Age*, explores the emotions, questions, struggles, and heartache filling my own life right now. Her beautiful, insightful writing will encourage all those caring for their parents at any level."

—**Kathy Howard**, Bible teacher, speaker, and author of *Lavish Grace*

"If you or someone you know has aging parents, this book is a must-read. Cynthia Ruchti offers a fresh perspective on the challenges and concerns those of us with aging parents face every day. Don't miss her compassionate insight, hope, and comfort during this time of changes and new choices."

—**Jackie M. Johnson**, author of *Power Prayers for Women*
and *Praying with Power When Life Gets Tough*

"*As My Parents Age* should be on the bookshelf of every person whose parents are getting older. Practical advice oozes from every story in a way that makes you say, 'Oh, I need to do that!' But it is not the advice that makes this book a must-read. It is the heart and hope that overflow from every page. It will help you serve your parents with grace and encourage you to make the most of times with your loved ones."

—**Linda Gilden**, author, speaker, and writing coach

As My Parents Age

Reflections on Life, Love, and Change

Cynthia Ruchti

WORTHY
Inspired

Published by Worthy Inspired, an imprint of Worthy Publishing Group, a division of Worthy Media, Inc., One Franklin Park, 6100 Tower Circle, Suite 210, Franklin, TN 37067.

WORTHY is a registered trademark of Worthy Media, Inc.

HELPING PEOPLE EXPERIENCE THE HEART OF GOD

eBook available wherever digital books are sold.

Library of Congress Cataloging-in-Publication Data

Names: Ruchti, Cynthia, author.
Title: As my parents age : reflections on life, love, and change / by Cynthia Ruchti.
Description: Franklin, TN : Worthy Publishing, 2017.
Identifiers: LCCN 2017005521 | ISBN 9781617957529 (tradepaper)
Subjects: LCSH: Aging--Religious aspects--Christianity. | Aging parents--Care--Religious aspects--Christianity. | Older persons--Religious life. | Caregivers--Religious life.
Classification: LCC BV4580 .R83 2017 | DDC 248.8/5--dc23
LC record available at https://lccn.loc.gov/2017005521

For foreign and subsidiary rights, contact rights@worthypublishing.com

ISBN: 978-1-61795-752-9

Cover Design: Jeff Jansen | Aesthetic Soup
Cover Photo: Shutterstock.com

Printed in the United States of America
17 18 19 20 21 LBM 9 8 7 6 5 4 3 2 1

*The author expresses her gratitude
to the people willing to share their stories
about caring for aging parents.
Some names and unessential details
were changed for privacy's sake.*

Contents

———⊗———

Into the mist of mind
The fog of memories lost
The blinding drifts of thought and soul
The gale of age's cost
We plunge, our shoulders hunched
Against the biting sting
We cling to
The ones we knew
When age was a "someday" thing.

Cynthia Ruchti

INTRODUCTION

In our tradition, it's expected we'll do everything we can for our elders. All the time."

An ancient thought from a long-lost civilization? A voice from a holy text? The first line of an assisted-living brochure? I jotted the quote on a scrap of paper as the television aired one of my husband's many survival/Alaska/adventure/Yukon/backwoods/northwoods/woods-of-any-kind favorite shows.

The words came from soft-spoken subsistence hunter Caribou Charlie's mouth on *Yukon Men*. He'd recently returned from an unplanned hunting trip, filled his freezer and pantry, and was in the middle of tackling an endless list of winterizing projects when his mother-in-law walked onto his property and quietly said, "I wonder if you would do me a favor." His mother-in-law had little meat to sustain her through the upcoming harsh winter months.

Charlie dropped everything he considered a priority for a higher calling—helping provide for his aging mother-in-law. "Everything we can for our elders. All the time."

It's not unlike the reminder God gave His people when they'd strayed from a millennia-old tradition of venerating and caring for the aged. The original concept traces back through so many cultures and eras that one could argue caring for the elderly is an inborn instinct. But in the years when Jesus walked the earth, that God-given instinct had been overridden by a too-familiar distortion of God's plan.

"We gave at the office," the religious said when confronted about their disregard for the ill and aging among them. They followed what they believed to be the most noble—and noticeable—of ancient teachings. They were diligent to give an exacting ten percent of everything, including leaves of mint and fronds of dill and gift bags of ground cumin. But Jesus called them out for neglecting aging members of their families, unimpressed by the religious leaders' perfectionism with herbs and spices.

The mint-minded missed the point. When it comes to caring for aging parents, we can't phone it in, although we can phone. We can't throw money at the problem, although we do have to invest, and some of that investment is in the form of dollars.

But this isn't a book about getting it right, about responding to the mandate to care for aging parents. You have shown you care by opening a book with a title like this one. Its pages are filled with stories of people like you who are already invested and running on empty—people who are weary, uncertain, frustrated, hurt, saddened, aching, overwhelmed, overloaded, underappreciated, torn between the needs of children and the needs of parents, tasked with making impossible choices, enjoying the time they have with their parents but shattered by how short-lived that time may be . . . or all of the above.

As you turn the pages, you may catch a line that temporarily lightens your load or find a fresh perspective that converts tough moments into tender memories. Or you'll breathe a little easier, having been reminded that you're not alone. Maybe you'll rediscover what you already know—that this season is hard, but your efforts don't go unnoticed by the God who called you to somehow—even or *especially* now—"honor your father and mother."

Despite our valiant efforts, the fact remains that we cannot stop the aging process. What we can do, with God's help, is ensure that we and those we love age as gracefully and graciously as possible.

You can read these chapters devotionally—one a day or one a week or when you can snatch a moment in a waiting room. Or you can read until your soul is refreshed and your reasons for pouring yourself out for your parents indelibly etched. Then you can return to the courage-builders from God's Word, the experiences of others on the path beside you, and a word or two from those who pair clinical wisdom with hard-fought compassion, until you feel bolstered and fortified for the next hard thing.

I'll pretend my mom is still reachable by phone and Dad is napping rather than long gone. We'll walk through this together.

We plunge, our shoulders hunched
Against the biting sting.
We cling to
The ones we knew
When age was a "someday" thing.

CHAPTER ONE

When I Notice the First Signs

Despite our valiant efforts,
we cannot stop the aging process.
But God never says,
"Whoa. I did not see that coming."

Although she might have disagreed, fashion sense ranked lower on the list of my mom's strengths and skill sets than my siblings and I would have liked. The good news is that no one could accuse her of trying to dress two decades younger than her age.

But the day she showed up at an event wearing avocado-green slacks with a kelly-green sweater, my sisters and I looked at each other as if we could hear the unspoken words that flew between us: "And . . . it begins."

Aging.

But it wasn't the beginning at all.

The aging process started when my grandmother pushed my mom out into the world. One minute *old*. Two weeks *old*. Four years *old*. Forty years *old*. The process continued for her until she drew her final breath of earth air at age eighty-three. She'd lived twenty-four years past the first of many heart attacks. She'd survived nine years of congestive heart failure, four years in a home hospice program, and nine months of "any minute now" in a hospice-residence facility.

For a long time after Mom died, the phone beside my bed unnerved me. I no longer had reason to lie awake listening for its ring in the night. No one would ever call to tell me that my mom needed me or she'd taken a turn for the worse. She was gone.

For her, the "as my parents age" phase lasted much longer than our family members imagined possible. It began as my mom uttered her first newborn cry—as it does for all of us—then intensified in her sixties, seventies, and eighties as her health grew progressively worse, and finally came to a quiet halt on a Monday afternoon seven years ago when God said, "Dorothy, that's quite enough. Come home."

Some say aging signals death's approach the way the first stray snowflake warns of winter's impending arrival. Others say aging signals a life well-lived. Or that aging is simply a new stage of living—an advanced stage of the human soul's life cycle.

Poetic.

Then why the flood of antiaging serums, pills, supplements, and creams? Why the frenzy to at least slow or mask the aging process if we can't stop it?

Most of us cope far better with the signs that *we're* aging than we do with the telltale signs that our parents are. In childhood, every new phase is a sign of growth and development, of new adventures and skills, newly realized potential and accomplishment. Progression in an elderly person usually means loss, decline, retired skills—relinquishing rather than attaining.

Our relationship with an aging parent changes, and not always for the better. The aging process slaps us in the face with its rude reminder that time with our beloved parent is fleeting. It has an end point. No matter when that date arrives, it will seem too soon.

Nothing we face—emotionally, physically, spiritually, financially, mentally—surprises God. Not even aging. It's a season He's watched His children traverse since Adam and Eve noticed their first wrinkles, since Eve plucked her first gray hair, noticed her skin was getting crepey and muttered, "'Eat the fruit,' the serpent said. 'What could happen?'"

American culture focuses on the negatives of aging. But many of the elderly—similar to the wild, stunning colors of autumn leaves prior to winter's approach—are taking advantage of the accompanying benefits. They're serving others, inventing new ministries, spending time with their grandchildren, or helping their middle-aged children through the "middles."

They travel—canes and walkers notwithstanding—to places that had been on their wish lists for too long. They're socializing, entertaining others, and choosing the pace at which they live rather than being forced into an unnatural pace by a job or other responsibilities.

The emotionally healthiest among them lace their days with laughter and friendships, mending fences that have served no real purpose. They convert from two-wheeled to three-wheeled motorcycles so they can still participate in their favorite pastimes. They take cooking classes. They learn languages they may never be called upon to use, simply for the joy of expanding their knowledge. In some cases, they're leaving grown children in the dust with their voracious appetites for risk-taking and attempting new things.

Part of the season when we watch our parents age may be hemmed in awe. We discover what really matters to our parents when the "have-tos" are stripped away. We re-connect with them on a new level—adult to adult—and step into a not-altogether-unpleasant role of meeting their needs in ways that weren't possible or necessary before. We enjoy shared goals and serve our communities side by side.

Until ill health or memory issues or the natural effects of advanced aging threaten to disturb that scene.

Solomon wrote poetically and soberly of that season in Ecclesiastes 12:1–7 (AMP):

> Remember [thoughtfully] also your Creator in the days of your youth [for you are not your own, but His], before the evil days come or the years draw near when you will say [of physical pleasures], "I have no enjoyment *and* delight in them"; before the sun and the light, and the moon and the stars are darkened [by impaired vision], and the clouds [of depression] return after the rain [of tears]; in the day when the keepers of the house (hands, arms) tremble, and the strong men (feet, knees) bow themselves, and the grinders (molar

teeth) cease because they are few, and those (eyes) who look through the windows grow dim; when the doors (lips) are shut in the streets and the sound of the grinding [of the teeth] is low, and one rises at the sound of a bird *and* the crowing of a rooster, and all the daughters of music (voice, ears) sing softly. Furthermore, they are afraid of a high place and of dangers on the road; the almond tree (hair) blossoms [white], and the grasshopper (a little thing) is a burden, and the caperberry (desire, appetite) fails. For man goes to his eternal home and the mourners go about the streets and market places. *Earnestly remember your Creator* before the silver cord [of life] is broken, or the golden bowl is crushed, or the pitcher at the fountain is shattered and the wheel at the cistern is crushed; then the dust [out of which God made man's body] will return to the earth as it was, and the spirit will return to God who gave it.

Aging. An inescapable reality, barring early death. Watching our parents age—also inescapable.

But we draw great fortifying breaths of comfort from knowing that God is not silent on the subject. He intends to accompany us on the journey, to catch us when we stumble, and to point out the can't-miss beauty along the way.

It cost him
But my father asked me
To climb the ladder
He's climbed all his life
To free the rain gutters
Of decaying leaves

And in that moment
I knew
I knew he would need me now
And that I had two choices

I could make a big deal
About the sacrifice of my time
Or I could make every step
Up that ladder
An expression of my love

I chose love.

CHAPTER TWO

When It All Comes Down to What Matters Most

How naively the toddler says,
"I can't wait to be older."

My mother was lucid for all of her eighty-three years. But near the end of her life, heavy-duty pain medication coupled with her limping heart brought moments of distress that exacerbated her anxiety and lifelong selective impatience. During her years as a nurse, she'd built a reputation for endless patience with her patients. We siblings mused that she must have spent her reserves of the grace, which left little of it for things like slow-moving trains, sluggish Internet connections, and God's timetable for her final breath.

Dependent upon those of us who lived close to her after Dad's premature death at sixty-four—right on time in God's eyes, no doubt, but premature to our way of thinking—Mom let the impatient side of herself slip out in observations about how often we should call or visit, how soon to flip on our turn signal when driving her to or from a doctor's appointment, and how inconvenient it was that the server at the Asian restaurant spoke her native language clearly, but only halting English.

Pain can intensify the smallest character quirk or flaw. We see it happening when we're down with the flu. Why would we be surprised to see it magnified when the pain is a deep emotional wound or the crushing pain that sometimes accompanies end-of-life illnesses for an aging parent?

As my mom neared her final days, she grew agitated about her Bible. When I walked into her room at the hospice residence facility one afternoon, her eyes showed her frustration: "Need to read it. I can't read it. Help me." She repeated, "Seventy-one. Seventy-one. Seventy-one."

My impulse was to remind her she'd passed seventy-one a dozen years earlier but then realized she was talking about a chapter or a verse or both. "What book of the Bible, Mom? I'll find it for you."

"Is it ninety-one? Ninety-one," she said, wringing scary-thin hands that had once been plump and strong.

I'd seen this dramatic level of agitation a few times since she'd grown too weak to hold a hairbrush or dress herself. It threatened my own beating heart's rhythm. My precious mother, a rock of stability with a little stubborn mixed in, helpless and frightened and desperate for something she couldn't define.

"In the Psalms, Mom?"

I started with Psalm 91, skimming first, noting truths that would comfort both of us in the room. Lines like, "Living in the Most High's shelter, camping in the Almighty's shade, I say to the Lord, 'You are my refuge, my stronghold! You are my God—the one I trust' " (Psalm 91:1–2 CEB) and "God will protect you with his pinions; you'll find refuge under his wings. His faithfulness is a protective shield" (verse 4). And "Don't be afraid of terrors at night, arrows that fly in daylight, or sickness that prowls in the dark, destruction that ravages at noontime" (verses 5–6).

She shook her head as violently as her almost-nonexistent energy would allow. "No, no, no."

What had I missed? Why wasn't her soul appeased by these ancient yet ever-new promises? I flipped back a few pages to Psalm 71, leaving the 91 her thoughts had eventually landed on.

I held her hand as I read the first few verses. They sounded a lot like a repeat of God's promises to those in a place of deep need—"Be my rock of refuge where I can always escape," (Psalm 71:3 CEB). Then my eyes caught up with her heart when I read verse nine: "Don't cast me off in old age. Don't abandon me when my strength is used up!" The words on the page blurred as I continued reading to the one who had first read stories to me.

> But me? I will hope. Always. . . . Lord, I will help others remember nothing but your righteous deeds. You've taught me since my youth, God, and I'm still proclaiming your wondrous deeds! So, even in my old age with gray hair, don't abandon me, God! Not until I tell generations about your mighty arm, tell all who are yet to come about your strength, and about your ultimate righteousness,

God. . . . You, who have shown me many troubles and calamities, will revive me once more (Psalm 71:14, 16–20 CEB).

The tension abated. My mom's soul—and mine—had cried out for reassurance that *the valley of the shadow* did not stretch into eternity. It had an end point. And in the meantime, the in-between time? She and I would cling to the Word that replaced agitation and impatience with peace.

Monica says, "I'm blessed because at almost fifty-eight years old, I still have both of my parents and they are able to remain at home. It is difficult to watch them slow down and [experience] all the other things that go with aging. But the most difficult thing is knowing I won't always have them in this life. That, someday, their chairs at the kitchen table will be empty."

Empty chairs.

Fodder for still-life artists, photographers, and book-cover designers. But for those with aging parents, an empty chair represents a stark relationship end point. Navigating toward that end point—whether it is too near or far in the distance—can't help but nudge us toward life's large and looming questions. Among them is this: "As my parents age, what matters most?"

How would you answer that? Does your thought follow one of these paths?

- It's time to iron out that wrinkle in our relationship. It's not worth holding on to that grudge in light of what lies ahead.
- We need to have the hard talks. Who will serve as their power of attorney or financial power of attorney? Are their wills up-to-date so their wishes will be clearly known? Do they have living wills for medical intervention? What are their thoughts now compared to when they were my age?
- How will my daily routine need to change to accommodate my parents' care?
- Are they spiritually and emotionally ready for that eventual end point? Am I?

Take a few moments now—the elusive "later" grows more elusive as time passes—to consider how you and your parents would answer the question, "At this season of life, what matters most to us as individuals and as a family?" And then spend another moment considering and praying over this verse, underlined in the pages of my mother's Bible: "Don't cast me off in old age. Don't abandon me when my strength is used up!" Psalm 71:9 (CEB).

Great God of comfort,
Inventor of faithfulness,
You who breathed our first breath for us
And will kiss away the last,
Steady us.
Strengthen us.
Surprise us
With old truths
Lit from within
By Your Spirit
As we embark on a journey
We didn't know we'd signed up for—
Watching our parents grow older.
And older. Or not.
In the name of Jesus,
Hope of all hopes,
Amen.

CHAPTER THREE

When They're Miles and Miles Away

The distance between a caring child and an aging parent
is infinitely farther than the map claims.

It's hard but good watching our children grow up; kids are supposed to grow up and move away. It can be hard, hard, hard watching our parents age. The inevitable end result is loss. And in the middle is a cluster of mini-losses. Change brought about by aging can be as challenging to witness as it is to experience.

"My father lay in the hospital across the country from me when he was sixty-four," my friend Tina noted. "His medical issues would have been beyond my ability to help even if I had been there. But trying to talk to him on the hospital phone as he lay dying? What a helpless feeling."

The following dialogue snippet may strike too close to home for you.

"Dad, you say 'I'm fine' every time I ask how you're doing. 'I'm fine.' I want to know the truth. How *fine* are you?"

"Would it matter how I answered? You live too far away to do anything about it."

Too many adult children of aging parents have had similar conversations. Distance from an aging or ill mother or father is considered one of the most potent sources of frustration during this period of life, according to those who have walked that path.

- I can't be there to hug her, even if there's nothing I can do to help ease her pain.
- Logically, I know it's my job or my spouse's job

or my parents' choice that keeps this distance of miles between us. But that doesn't prevent guilt from disturbing the peace.

- I don't know how much he's hiding from me because he doesn't want me to worry. Ironically, that's the source of my *greatest* level of worry.

- Seeing my parents so infrequently makes it shocking to notice the decline. How did that happen? When? Why wasn't I there? As if I could have prevented them from aging.

- I don't want a call from the hospital or the funeral home to be the first clue I have about how "not fine" Dad was all this time.

Charity talked to her mother every Thursday evening on the phone. Her mother's voice sounded subdued, but nothing obvious warned that trouble brewed. One holiday visit, Charity noticed her mom's "immaculate" apartment no longer qualified for that status. Mail from weeks earlier lay unopened in a basket on the counter. Several scorched pans showed evidence that burners had been left on too long—or forgotten entirely. But her mom insisted she was doing okay and had been unusually busy preparing for their visit.

Before they said uneasy good-byes and prepared to make the cross-country trip at the end of the holiday weekend, Charity and her husband set up the necessary technology so she and her mom could share video calls. They left a laminated recipe card of instructions for the older woman to follow.

The visual connection helped for a few weeks. Then Charity's mom claimed it was "too much fuss," and refused to communicate any way other than by phone.

"The distance felt as if it had grown from two thousand miles to twenty thousand," Charity said. "I knew there were things she didn't want me to see on the video. I assumed she was ashamed that she'd let the house go, even though Ben and I insisted we'd find a way to pay for a cleaning lady if it would help her. In the end, it was far more than that. When my next visit was at the urging of her doctor, I found her covered in deep purple bruises—a combination of poor nutrition, prescription misuse, and a series of falls she hadn't reported. If I had known. . . ."

Video-chat capabilities weren't readily available when my mom was aging. As a nurse and a rarely wrong diagnostician, she had taught us what to watch for in skin color, breath sounds, pupil dilation, fluid retention, and my favorite—"pitting edema." Using video chat, my siblings and I could have tracked her eye movements and facial tics or noticed the all-too-familiar droop of her jaw that signaled another heart attack. She lived fifteen minutes away. At times, it still seemed too far. I can't imagine the heart trauma of people like Charity, caring about an aging parent who lives what feels like a world away.

Whether it's parents aching to know what's going on in their college student's life on campus or parents holding their breath through a child's deployment or those children now grown and concerned about their aging parents' health, distance prevents us from protecting those we love. It always has.

But distance is no challenge for God. He sees both us and them without having to turn His divine head. He hears our pleas and theirs with equal acuity. And He remains our strongest advocate when parents live far away.

You may have found it *too* comfortable to have distance between you and an aging parent. Caught up in the barrage of daily duties and the pressure of surviving your own work, family, financial, or health issues, the distance makes it all too easy to relegate thoughts of your aging parents to "I should call Dad one of these days" or "I wonder how Mom's tests turned out."

We can put systems in place, call our parents more frequently, enlist the aid of neighbors to check on them, take turns with our siblings or other relatives, and make the long trek to see for ourselves, but no one has a 24/7 view of our parents and our aching hearts the way God does.

That knowledge may not change the circumstances, but it can change our perspective. His love spans distances we can't manage. It also changes the way we pray for those we love but can't touch.

Through prayer, you can have an impact even if you aren't close enough to look into their eyes. God is. He hears. And He responds to prayers spoken in sincere faith. Get specific about your parents' possible prayer needs. Write out your thoughts in a notebook or journal or on your computer or in your phone.

Pray for caring friends who will tell them the truth in love, for companionship that lifts their spirits, for wisdom about their limitations, and for restored relationships. Ask God to gift them with the ability to maintain a sense of adventure despite limitations and to find sound financial advice and trustworthy medical professionals.

Pray for a safe and soul-refreshing place to live and for peace about the future.

Father God,
Wrap Your arms around my mom tonight.
Help my daddy hear Your voice clearly
When everything else around him
seems utterly confusing.
Remind them that they are included
in the 'you' in Your promise
"Never will I leave you. Never will I forsake you"
(Hebrews 13:5 NIV).
In the strong name of the One
for whom distance is no hindrance, amen.

CHAPTER FOUR

When We Mourn and Embrace the Role Reversal

We can't make ourselves feel grander
by making our parents appear smaller.

I say I lost my mom on a certain date in November 2015," my friend Tricia told me. "But that's not accurate. The date marked the last of a string of losses that began many years earlier, soon after she was diagnosed. All the little losses added up to the big emptiness of her leaving me for heaven."

Tricia described how so many of the activities that had bonded them all their lives faded away, one by one, as her mother became weaker and disinterested. Her mother grew—as many do—more helpless, dependent, and frail. "I eventually had to bathe her. We used the tub in which she'd bathed her children over the years. Every time I assisted her into the tub and took that washcloth to clean her skin, I would thank God for the sacred grace. It was overwhelming to bathe my mother's frail, weak body. That she would let me do it and receive the help graciously was by far the most tender experience of my life."

I remember similar moments with my mom and also when my husband went through a season of needing my full-time assistance for the simplest of his physical needs.

"I care. Let me help you." The words can be met with a variety of responses, some heartbreaking.

A toddler says, "No! I can do it myself!"

A teen says, "I don't want . . . or need . . . your help."

A mature adult says, "Thanks. I could use it."

Aging parents could respond in any of those three

ways on any given day. Their emotional fluctuations may be governed by mood, pain, confusion, disorientation, frustration, shame, remorse, loss of dignity, fear for the future. . . . Parents may say exactly what they mean—"I don't want your help"—or the opposite of what they mean.

Our human drive for independence starts young. With only brief interruptions, it continues and often intensifies as we mature. But part of the fallout of our later years is the dreaded loss of independence. The mother who once fed and clothed her children now requires similar help from those same children. The father who taught his sons to change a tire now depends on them to transport him to medical appointments. In the early stages of role reversal, the loss of independence may be slight and seem insignificant to us but loom large in our parents' eyes.

"Mom, are you eating enough?"

"Dad. Dad? You left your keys in the door."

"It's not a big deal, Mom. I forget names at times too."

Our desire to help isn't always met with a response that seems logical, much less grateful. But wasn't it like that when the one we sought to help was a young child? And what did we do then? We leaned on God's wisdom to tell us if it was time to press through and help anyway or step back and give the child a chance to try.

Those who care for parents expressing gratitude for the kindnesses shown them—sometimes *sacrificial* kindnesses that have taken us far out of our way or our comfort limits—find that gratitude fuels energy for more caregiving. A grateful parent—like a grateful child—adds the element of tenderness my friend Tricia saw marking her relationship with her ailing mother.

Try a little tenderness. It's not just a thought a lyricist invented last century. It's a way of life proposed by the God who knew we would face seasons that naturally lack tenderness, who knew we'd need the reminder.

Tricia applied the tenderness philosophy to the mounting difficulties she encountered as connections she shared with her mother disintegrated. No more shopping together. No more shared jokes—her mother had forgotten her half. No more letting conversations wander wherever they wanted to go. No more annual mother-daughter retreats. No more dependence on her mother's embrace and wisdom when Tricia was hurting—her mother hurt more. No more admitting to her mother how much she needed her. It would have caused her mother greater distress.

"The most tender moment I had with my late eighty-three-year-old dad," my friend Jackie said, "was when I had to leave all my sons and their families, including all my grandchildren, my husband, my home, and my dog behind in Ohio to travel to South Carolina to help my dad move back there. But he became ill and could no longer be alone. The month the trip was supposed to take turned into a little over a year, with me as his caregiver. One day he looked over at me and said 'Thank you. No one else would have done this for me.'"

"I treasure those words," Jackie said. "He was always a very independent person. I know how hard it was for him to lose his health and mobility. He was always my hero and I miss him, but I am grateful for that year we had together."

What's at the core of our resistance to serve as caregivers for our aging parents—whether in a full-time capacity or in small role-reversal ways? Have you wrestled with any of these joy-stealing thoughts?

- It's an intrusion on my life plan. Just when the pieces are coming together for me to enjoy a little freedom—just as the nest is emptying and my kids don't need me so heavily—now my parents do. I hate to admit it. I love my parents. But their needs are intrusive.

- Psychologically, I don't like seeing my parents so dependent on me. And I'm sure they don't derive pleasure from needing me as much as they do.

- My life is full. The stress I'm managing cannot take one more hit.

- I want to help. I have no clue how. Every attempt is apparently the opposite of what they really need.

- I'm afraid. There. I said it. I don't want to lose

the relationship we had when we stood on equal footing.

- My parents haven't been easy to get along with. Ever. I dread this season. Does that make me unredeemable?

- Their needing me couldn't have come at a worse time. Just being honest. My career is finally taking off.

Statements like the above aren't linked to a lack of love. In fact, love for our parents often makes confessing those core issues so guilt-laden that we don't admit them to anyone, even to ourselves.

Others of us find the role reversal far less of a system shock. We're divinely gifted for it, expecting it, prepared and blessed by the opportunity to serve our parents.

No matter what motivation is at work beneath the surface, we can know God's will in the matter.

"But if anyone does not provide for his relatives, and especially for members of his household, he has denied the faith," says 1 Timothy 5:8 (ESV).

"'Honor your father and mother' (this is the first commandment with a promise), 'that it may go well with you and that you may live long in the land'" (Ephesians 6:2–3 ESV).

The only questions that remain are, "How?" And "How, in this unique season?"

Lord God,
When what You ask of me
In caring for my parents
Creates discomfort,
Remind me
That love
And sacrifice
Are practically synonymous
And that
On that score too,
You
Paved
The
Way.

CHAPTER FIVE

When My Children Need Me Too

*God would not call us to a task that requires us
to neglect what He's already assigned to us.*

I hate having to tell my parents I can't be there for them," Ron said. "But sometimes it's unavoidable. My wife and I tag team the best we can. We've even taken separate vacations so that one of us is here for my live-in elderly parents' needs."

Whose needs come first? No matter how diligent we are to maintain a healthy balance, no matter how skilled we get at involving others in sharing the load, God is the only One who can help us determine whose needs take priority at any given moment.

"I'm caught in the middle, the knot in the center of a tug-of-war for my time and attention. I'm either short-changing my immediate family or my extended family . . . or my church . . . or my job . . . or myself," Cathy said.

Unique seasons of life call for unique solutions, relinquishing preconceived ideas of how much we can handle on our own.

Some equate the season of caring for aging parents with the stresses related to having a newborn in the house. But it may be more like having quintuplets in the house, because the juggling act of responsibilities is intensified.

Many who care for aging parents express frustration that the needs of their parents almost seem in competition with the needs of their children. They don't want to think that way. But the idea of being sandwiched between the needs is not a catchphrase. It's reality.

What's intriguing is that blending the two contrasting caregiving opportunities may provide a partial solution—and more than a few teachable moments.

Here's Sandra's story:

"Years ago, when my beloved grandmother 'Mama Farley' died at age ninety, my husband, Don, and I decided our five-year-old daughter, Holly, and six-year-old son, Jay, would attend the Kentucky funeral with us. During the long drive, we talked about heaven and told our children that Mama—the part we couldn't see—was already with the Lord.

"Then I, a veteran of Southern funerals, told about the part they *would* see. She'd be lying in a big box called a casket, surrounded by flowers. A lot of people would be in the room, I said, and many would be crying because Mama Farley couldn't talk to them anymore. I talked about the sad hymns the people would sing, what the minister would say, and even about the procession to the cemetery after her adult grandsons carried the casket to the big car called a hearse.

"Then, most important of all, I asked if they had any questions. Jay wondered about practical matters, such as how they would put the casket into the ground, but Holly just stared at me, her eyes round with silent wonderings.

"When we arrived at the funeral home, we held the

children's hands and walked into the flowered area. I studied Mama Farley's dear, ancient face and thought of the godly example she'd been. Lost in my memories, I was startled by Holly's whispered question: 'Is she breathing?'

"I hadn't anticipated a question like that, and it required more than just a quick 'No, of course not.' Suddenly this business of explaining death even to myself had become difficult. How could I help a child grasp what I couldn't?

"'Well, Holly . . . ,' I stalled, searching for something both simple and theologically sound.

"Jay turned from studying the casket handles to face his little sister. 'No, Holly, she's not breathing. Remember? The breathin' part's in heaven.'

"Since that long-ago April day, I've stood before all too many caskets. But even with tears running down my cheeks, I am comforted as I remember a little voice confidently announcing, 'The breathin' part's in heaven.'"

Weaving children into the entire life cycle can make life so much richer than keeping their care and the care of aging parents separate.

"Even though she was 'feeling her age,' my mother-in-law took my daughter one day and taught her how to make her cinnamon rolls from scratch," Carmen said. "She wanted to be sure to pass on that tradition."

Some of the most well-adjusted young people I know

are those who see themselves as part of an extended family—the very young and the very old. They find their rhythm within the pulse of the family as a whole and understand better than most where their needs fit during any given moment.

We wrestle with thinking it's an all-or-nothing game. "If I can't be there for my child's every breath or if I can't be there for my parent's every sigh," we think, "I'm failing on both counts." But that's not how life's rhythm operates. It's syncopated and varied, with fast and slow passages, crescendos and decrescendos, youthful needs combined with needs of the elderly.

Is it difficult music to master? Well, not everyone masters it. But we keep practicing.

Life will hand us plenty of practice time.

It shouldn't come as a surprise to any of us that the needs of aging parents would dovetail with the needs of our careers and our growing children. Math can tell us that much. Our preparation for that season of life is simpler than we might assume.

It's directly related to our surrender to the rhythms of grace, to walking moment by moment according to the precise direction of the Spirit of God. With our eyes on the Director's baton, we will find priorities aligning, sometimes colliding, and then resolving into a pattern as harmonious as possible when aging is the issue.

"Then the way you live [including caregiving decision-making] will always honor and please the Lord, and your lives will produce every kind of good fruit [as you serve both your children and your parents]. All the while, you will grow as you learn to know God better and better" (Colossians 1:10 NLT, bracketed material mine).

My parents
Or my children,
God?
The question never ends.
Which one needs me most
Right now?
Which is more important?
How can I ever know for sure?

My Child,
Do you think I know all things?
Even this?

Yes, Lord.

Then here's an idea.
Follow My lead.

CHAPTER SIX

When My Parents Won't Accept Help

There's an art to helping people
without making them feel bad
about needing our help.

Accepting help is a gift.

"My grandmother had very long hair," Connie said, "but it was thin, so she usually wore it in a bun with hair combs to keep it tidy. She would often let me take her hair down and brush it, and she always fell asleep. I was only twelve when she died. She's been gone for many years, but I still can feel the joy she gave me by letting me fix her hair. Since she was a farmwife, I may have been her only hairstylist."

Accepting help—a gift. Something to note when our turn comes.

My mother's independent spirit reached epic proportions after she was widowed at sixty-five. Over the course of her long illness, bits of independence fell away like pieces of shale on an unstable cliff. Asking for help didn't come naturally to her. It often came through gritted teeth after she'd endangered herself trying to manage a project beyond her strength. The times she refused our help or couldn't wait for assistance added more stressors to an already-stress-heavy situation.

On one level, we understood how important it was for her to stay independent. Removing layers of independence is like ripping dead skin from a severe sunburn. It's raw and tender underneath.

But our concern for her health and safety made us wish it were easier for her to ask for our help. Her three daughters and a number of grown grandchildren lived within just a few miles. When we'd find out after the fact that she could have used our help in rerouting her apartment full of oxygen tubing or retrieving a heavy box from a shelf in her closet, it was all too easy for our caring to be tinged with resentment that she didn't ask for help.

A few months ago, I had opportunity to test the theory that asking for help and graciously receiving it can bless all parties involved.

"You won't have to do a thing," my daughter said. "We'll bring all the food."

The topic was a holiday meal—traditionally held here in our one-hundred-year-old farmhouse, which has been the only homestead our three grown children have ever known. It's not fancy. It leans a little toward the center chimney. It has a small dining room, which means that once you're seated on the far side of the table, there's no moving until everyone peels out in order. But it's home. And cozy. And familiar. It's the gathering place, even though our children and grandchildren all live within fifteen miles of us right now. Yes, I know how blessed we are.

I was immersed in a tight deadline and fighting a knee that needed surgery—hence the offer for my children to provide all the holiday meal items. It was so kind of them to suggest it. I would have been a fool to refuse to let them step in and help.

How long will it be before they're making a similar offer and deadlines aren't the problem? Will I accept as graciously when their reasons are because I can't tell the difference between salt and sugar? Because I don't have the strength to lift the crescent rolls from the oven, much less the turkey? Or because they can't trust me to remember how many places to set at the table?

Over the years, I've witnessed the aging process in my mother and my in-laws, in my aunts and uncles, neighbors, and friends. And one day, I too will join the ranks of the rapidly aging. The aging process starts with life's first breath, so I more than qualify.

Whether the helper or the helpee, grace is our only hope. Hope is our saving grace. Statisticians tell us that as many as 90 percent of us will serve as a caregiver at least once in our lifetimes. Many of us will also be the recipient of caregivers' efforts. If we're graced with long life, we may well hear words like, "Let me do that for you. Let me help you. Please let me help."

It's an easy leap from that thought to the lesson handed down from Scripture, "Do unto others as you would have them do unto you." A modern paraphrase words it this way: "Here is a simple, rule-of-thumb guide for behavior: Ask yourself what you want people to do for you, then grab the initiative and do it for *them*. Add up God's Law and Prophets and this is what you get" (Matthew 7:12 MSG).

Not "as they *did* to you," but "as you want them to do for you."

When my mother's needs overwhelmed both of us, I leaned on that verse. It pointed me to a spot in the future where I'd be the one needing help. How would I hope my children would respond to me? With kindness, understanding, patience, joy, thoughtfulness . . . as if inconveniences can be and are always eclipsed by love.

It's a good thing. Because in caring for an aging adult, both the giving and the receiving are easier to accept if love is calling the shots. It's a delicate dance—offering and sometimes insisting on our help while maintaining our parents' desperate need for dignity and an inborn or culturally influenced self-sufficiency. Have you mastered the technique yet? I could use more practice.

"You all would do well to provide for their journey in a way that honors God," reads 3 John 6 (CEB).

That verse from John's letter to his friend Gaius—recorded in the Bible as the book of Third John—was intended to encourage Gaius to welcome coworkers for the cause of Christ, even if strangers. But the core principle landed softly on my heart regarding the subject of caring for aging parents.

An aging parent's journey—through the maze of aging itself and toward the end of life—presents challenges at every turn. The route is rarely smooth and eventless;

the ground underfoot is no longer flat and easily naviga-ble. Skin is no longer the armor it once was, sloughing off and bruising with the most minor of injuries. The journey seems dimly lit, and provisions are scarce. But the elder one is compelled to journey forward. Life demands it.

God and heaven are calling.

This is our task—to provide for their journey in a way that honors God. How? What does that mean? And—you might ask—what distinguishes *my* parents' journey from others?

What does the sojourner need? Companionship. Understanding. Physical provision. Emotional support. Guidance. Love. Shelter. Practical help with everything from calculating the cost to finding needed tools to a body-guard to protect from predators to shade from the scorch-ing heat. And the sojourner needs a reason to press on.

It's an incomplete list, and the degree of need or the specifics—one parent wants time, another wants space—vary widely from family to family, individual to individual, and even moment to moment.

How do we handle it?

If I had it to do over again, I would print this verse and hang it where I could see it every day: "Provide for their journey in a way that honors God."

"Guide me, O Thou great Jehovah"
Once sounded like
A cry for You
To illuminate *my* path, God.

Today it leaves my lips
As a plea
For You to guide me
In the best ways
To accompany
My parents
On *their* journeys
While deftly navigating mine
And conducting myself
In such a way
That they're grateful
For the company
And I'm grateful
For the privilege.

CHAPTER SEVEN

When I'm Tempted to Help Too Much

*God, help me understand
the difference between honoring my parents
and taking over.*

Neighbors at the cancer-care house where Xochitl's mother resided shared a small feast with Xochitl and her mom on a day they desperately needed a break. In return, her mother insisted on creating a thank-you dinner for them.

"As my mom gathered the ingredients for that meal, her humming bounced off the gray walls of the community kitchen," Xochitl reports. "I pressed my lips together as I diced onions, chopped bell peppers, and minced cilantro, but eventually I spoke up. 'You're not supposed to cook, Mom. Doctor's orders.'"

Her mother's hands, weakened by her treatments, trembled as she lifted the lid of the slow cooker. "Finish cutting those vegetables and stop nagging," she said.

When her mother reached to open the cupboard next to the stove, Xochitl dropped her knife, wiped her hands on a kitchen towel, and rushed to her mother's side. "Let me help you."

"I can do this." She let her hand rest on her daughter's shoulder. "I need to."

Xochitl loosened her grip and set the frying pan from the cupboard onto the stove. "I'm sorry."

"You know you miss my cooking."

"I do." She missed allowing herself to need her mom's comfort too.

"Placing my hand over hers," Xochitl wrote, "I rubbed her soft skin and swallowed an all-too-familiar longing for the simpler times before Mom's bone-marrow transplant. 'You'd better get busy sautéing those veggies, then.'"

Her mother's eyes glistened. "And you can check the pork. This time."

As our parents age, it's inevitable that we'll face moments when our desire to protect them interferes with their need to be who they are, to maintain their grip on their skills and interests, to be alive, vital, adventuresome, clever—and to prove it.

You may have heard the term "helicopter parenting" in a news report about hovering parents. It refers to "a style of parents who are overfocused on their children," says Carolyn Daitch, PhD, director of the Center for the Treatment of Anxiety Disorders near Detroit. "They typically take too much responsibility for their children's experiences and, specifically, their successes or failures," Dr. Daitch says.

It doesn't take much imagination to translate that into the realm of aging parents. Our caring about them and our desire to protect them can press us into overdrive. We cringe at the endless list of concerns for our aging parents' safety, protection from predatory financial advisors or relatives or both, dangers that sound similar to our warnings to toddlers. "Don't touch that. You'll get burned!" "Be careful with that." "Watch your step." "You need to eat more." "Here, let me do that for you."

Will we helicopter parent our aging parents? An occupational or physical therapist might watch our attempts to do things for our parents and advise, "Please don't let your desire to help turn into taking over for your parent. Stand by while they try. The length of time it takes will threaten your efficiency-expert mind-set. But the success will accomplish much more than the mere task itself. Serve as a spotter, not as a substitute, unless their health or safety is at stake."

Few children would learn to ride bicycles if Dad never stopped hanging on, providing an artificial source of balance.

Few of us would have learned how to use chopsticks if someone consistently ripped them from our hands and said, "Oh, for Pete's sake. Here's a fork."

Few of us would have gained a sense of accomplishment in any task if we hadn't been afforded the opportunity to try.

Even professional gymnasts use protective mats and spotters. But they're allowed to attempt the back flip. They're allowed to fail, over and over, always with help nearby and a watchful eye on their progress.

There's no denying that it's different with aging parents. They're not young and agile. Their bones don't heal easily if they slip and fall. But are there times when we need to sit down and ask our parents what level of help they'd like from us.

"Do you want me to open this box for you, Dad?" (Do you want me to serve as your spotter?)

"Would it help if I made it a point to water your plants each week, Mom? Or do you want to do that? And if you do, I have an idea for a system that will mean you don't have to carry that heavy watering can around the house."

A neighbor lady is housebound and in need of a great deal of physical help, but she wants to remain in her home for as long as possible. So her children have installed tools and aids throughout the house to help her retain her independence. Her children's help didn't come through helicoptering, but by equipping her to do as much as she can on her own.

Frequently, she'll report something new they discovered that will make her life easier but allow her the freedom she appreciates. An electric jar opener. A cupholder and basket that attach to her walker so she can carry her dinner to the porch on nice evenings. A longer chain for the fan over her kitchen table so she doesn't have to reach up.

Her children think creatively, protecting and aiding, but helping her most by enabling her to remain as independent as possible.

Love compels us—a good thing. But we still need wisdom to guide us. Our protective instincts can backfire and either scar the very ones we're trying to protect physically and emotionally or accelerate their decline.

How will we know? How will we ever know we're getting it right—loving, caring, and shielding without over-controlling or hurting more than we're helping?

Those answers may come in part from the professional caregivers or medical staff who advise us about what our parents need most from us. But ultimately, our strongest cues will come—on this subject as with all other decisions in life—from our connection to "the only wise God."

"Now to the King eternal, immortal, invisible, the only wise God, be honour and glory for ever and ever. Amen," says 1 Timothy 1:17 (KJV). "To the only wise God our Saviour, be glory and majesty, dominion and power, both now and ever. Amen"—Jude 1:25 (KJV). "To the only wise God be glory forever through Jesus Christ! Amen!" Romans 16:27 (NIV).

His wisdom is an attribute we can't live without in our season of second-guessing in caring for aging parents.

Are our decisions about our aging parents the best choices for them and for us? Those who follow tight on

Jesus's heels, who choose to stay tuned to what His Spirit is saying deep within us, find His wisdom rubbing off on us. It's bound to happen when we follow anyone that closely.

The benefit of the counsel of the only wise God is beyond calculating when what's at stake is our parents' health, dignity, and comfort—and our peace of mind.

God of all
Only wise God
I'm feeling my humanness more acutely
As my parents increasingly need me
But I still need them.

You who sees what I can
And what I can't
Help me listen for Your direction
Your whispered cues
So I don't misstep
Trying to keep them from falling.

CHAPTER EIGHT

When My Siblings Disagree on Our Parents' Care

Will we honor the cry on many parents' lips
regarding their children?
"Please love each other when I'm gone."

As if watching our parents age isn't already fraught with challenges, too often the situation is complicated by warring siblings. "Dad needs to get a different doctor. That one doesn't know what he's talking about." "You're coddling Mom. Let her do it herself." "You're never here to help. Why should I listen to you?" "Dad is not going to a nursing home." "His care is too much for any of us." "If you loved him, you'd let him stay with you. You work at home. We all have jobs." Bickering over differing opinions can quickly escalate into division and estrangement.

Few decisions on behalf of aging parents are uncomplicated. Valeri said, "Every decision for Mom was a battleground, every option a threat to our unity as a family."

Rachel and her brother were tasked with caring for their widowed mother as she aged. Other siblings offered nothing—from Rachel's perspective—except their criticism. They berated the two caregivers and yet let them handle the entire responsibility, all the sacrifice, all the labor, without a word of thanks.

An all-too-familiar story. A family crisis brings out the best or the worst in us. Too often, the worst. Remorse and frustration over not contributing—or being in a position that makes family members unable to contribute—erupts in harsh, hurtful critiques about what's being done by those who are present and hands-on. Communication breaks down when the overburdened and exhausted hands-on helpers fail to keep other family members informed. Opinion-glutted and answerless siblings foster a dynamic that, unless it's brought into balance, can fracture families.

It's a pattern witnessed since the invention of the family—arguing over the right thing to do and which sibling is responding correctly to the need. Cain and Abel weren't immune, and they were offspring of the first two humans—humans who knew what it was like to walk side by side with God.

David's brothers ridiculed him for the way he chose to serve those in need.

Joseph's brothers weren't shy about demonstrating their jealousy for the close relationship Joseph had with his father.

Even Jesus's disciples—more like brothers than friends—fought over which of them was favored above the others and who deserved His attention and His rewards. When Jesus was in physical danger, some ran. Some stayed but kept their distance. Some lashed out. Some denied they knew Him. Sounds like an unhealthy family, doesn't it?

Distress between siblings when a family member is in need is as old as history. More ancient than that is the wisdom of God and His transformational love.

"How wonderful and pleasant it is when brothers live together in harmony! For harmony is as precious as the anointing oil that was poured over Aaron's head, that ran down his beard and onto the border of his robe. Harmony is as refreshing as the dew from Mount Hermon that falls on the mountains of Zion. And there the LORD has pronounced his blessing, even life everlasting" (Psalm 133 NLT).

That's not the picture many families present when caring for aging parents. You've heard the admonitions:

- The family that plays together stays together.
- The family that prays together stays together.
- The family that camps/hunts/works/eats/ worships/bakes together stays together.

When aging parents change the family dynamic, the family that finds a way to talk it out respectfully and discovers a good balance of the emotional and physical workload stays together.

An equal division of labor may be a pipe dream. In what family are all the siblings equally gifted in peacemaking, comfort, administration, patience, physical strength . . . ? Most families recognize "Ben's the peacemaker. Barry's the numbers guy. Sheila has enough patience for all of us.

Suzanne is the planner. Sasha is strong in empathy. Brad is the get-it-done brother."

When my mother lay dying—even now, writing those words clutches at my heart—my two brothers and two sisters and I played different roles, of necessity. The brother who lived farthest away spent hours on the phone with Mom. Another brother and his wife—also a distance away—were faithful to send cards and notes.

The three daughters who lived closest each had their roles. One ran more errands than another. One had the financial means to provide tangible supplies. One of us cooked salt-free meals for her. My sister Jean lived and worked within blocks of Mom's apartment and, later, the hospice residence. So her physical presence clocked more hours than the rest of us, even though we were less than a half hour away. Two of us had some medical background, so we were the ones to notice when she exhibited signs of distress or discomfort.

It was important that we respected each others' unique gifts and methods of accompanying Mom on her journey, including my sister Carol—whose job and related responsibilities often kept her from visiting Mom as often as she wanted, but who was blessed to be the one to record Mom's last restless night of final words.

Our family dynamic was healthy before Mom's illness. It grew stronger through the long years of her suffering.

We attribute that to the grace of God, love for one another, and the respect we had for each other's contributions.

Despite the tight confines of her small apartment and later her hospice residence room, she was happiest when we were all together. All her children and grandchildren crammed into the room, using oxygen she needed. But she didn't care.

Only recently have I come to understand why it was so important for her to see us all together. She loved watching us love one another.

"Please love each other when I'm gone." Mom often expressed that emotion-packed longing, even though she knew it was probably unnecessary to tell us.

That's a promise to her that's been easy to keep.

Father God, hold our hands
As our parents age
So we clench no fists
But link arms.

Father God, hold our lips
As our parents age
So we spit no words
That build regret.

Father God, hold our hearts
As our parents age
So we risk no breach
In our family's fortress.

Father God, hold our attitudes
As our parents age
So we love well
Those our parents cherish.

CHAPTER NINE

When My Parents Won't Have the Hard Conversations

Love doesn't shy away from the difficult.
Love prefaces the difficult with the invitation,
"Lean on me."

I wish I could tell stories of caring for my father when he was elderly, of watching my brilliant, loving, faith-filled father age. But I can't. My paternal grandfather died at thirty-nine. My dad outlived that lifespan by two and a half decades. But when the middle-of-the-night call rang through the house in which I was a guest while attending a conference and I overheard the homeowner say, "I'll get her," I knew the call was for me. I knew it was bad news. I somehow knew it was about my dad. I knew he was gone. Too soon. Too soon. He'd had heart issues. We'd thought the issues were under control, until he woke my mom with the words, "Dot, I think I'm in trouble."

His death gutted the family and shocked the community. But our grief didn't shred our hearts. It tenderized them. It may have been the memory of losing his father so young or my dad's eagerness to see the Savior he'd served so faithfully all his adult life. He lived ready, as if perpetually "on call"—the ultimate call. No unfinished business. No unspoken words of encouragement. No unexpressed love.

And he'd already had The Conversation with me and my siblings. How had Dad and I passed the agonizing hours in the waiting room while Mom underwent emergency heart surgery two years prior? We had planned *his* funeral, to the smallest detail.

The list of hymns he wanted incorporated into his memorial service—which at the time we thought was far in the future—filled the paper on which I took notes as he mused. "Dad, in this country, funerals normally don't last for a week. Can we cut down this list to the bare essential hymns?"

He smiled and left the list as it was.

My father teared up as he named his favorite Scripture passages and said he preferred a closed casket when his time came. His faith in Jesus promised him an even more vibrant life after his current experience on earth. He wanted the focus on eternity, not on a used-up shell of a body.

We talked for hours in that small waiting room, threading our conversations about heaven and what awaits God-followers among prayers for my mom and the surgeons working to save her life.

Planning Mom's funeral would have been morbid and defeatist. Instead, we planned his.

Minutes after the middle-of-the-night call that told me he was gone, I lay across my borrowed bed, listening to the train in the distance, certain my life would never again be the same with my father missing from it. I was right.

I couldn't get a ride from the conference location to my mom's house until morning. But sleep would occupy none of the moments until then.

Peace and agony in one package. He was gone. He knew I loved him. I knew he loved me. He was gone, but we'd left nothing unsaid.

We'd had The Conversation. In detail. The family members knew he didn't fear death, whether it came quickly or delayed. We knew what was on his heart regarding the gathering of friends and family to pay their final respects. We knew the hymns he wanted and the verses we could skip . . . which was none of them.

Mom had recovered from the emergency surgery during which Dad and I talked about hard things. In fact, she lived twenty more years. She too made her wishes known. She contracted with the local funeral home that would handle the arrangements when the time came. Who but God knew she'd have to update her carefully crafted obituary a dozen times before it was needed?

The family joked that Mom and the funeral director were on a first-name basis. On any random day, Mom might list her activities as:

- Pick up strawberries at the farmers' market.
- Get my prescription refilled for the nitroglycerin pills.
- Stop by Carl's to update the casket package. (Her first-choice casket option had gone out of style while she waited for The Moment.)

Some families find it awkward to discuss funeral plans, financial decisions, who gets what, and preferred casket linings, burial plots, or ash-scattering locations. Our family considered it a gift that we didn't have to wonder how to honor our parents. They'd told us their wishes ahead of time.

And we'd heard from their mouths that they faced death without fear.

When Mom's extended battle with congestive heart failure rendered her too weak to make decisions, we all rested in the peace that key decisions had been made long ago. We focused instead on surrounding her with a cocoon of love as she approached her final breath.

"If we don't talk about it, maybe we can keep it from happening." Isn't that the unspoken hope many families entertain?

Postponing The Conversation won't prevent the need for it.

How do we tackle the impossible tasks in life? How does one survive the humiliating experiences? How do we press through the things that seem beyond us . . . including having The Conversation?

Nursing home/assisted living/in-home hospice care, getting the will in order, dividing possessions, end-of-life issues, power of attorney, living will, moving in. . . .

We navigate difficult discussions—even these—speaking truth couched in love, as God instructs in Ephesians 4:15. We create an atmosphere in which even conversations about the end of life or its approach fall softly on ears and hearts.

One of the secrets is not waiting until end of life seems imminent. In some cultures, it might seem a bad omen to discuss such things before then. Or at all. But I have yet to meet a family that could openly discuss end-of-life issues who regretted having those talks. Instead, talking about the hard things brought a deep sense of peace, especially to families of faith that had no fears about what happens after death.

It's an easy talk to postpone. But doing so can create a breeding ground for disappointment, misunderstanding, and confusion, in addition to chaos, should the need for that information come before the family is ready.

Hard conversations? They're harder if they never take place.

God of inextinguishable light
And life,
May Your love
Pave the path
We must travel
To meet at the conversation table
To talk about
Unspeakable things
That serve as prelude
To the life
Of unending joy.

CHAPTER TEN

When They Can't Let Old Hurts Go

The most effective antiaging solution
is a heart free from bitterness.

A calm and undisturbed mind and heart are the life and health of the body, but envy, jealousy, and wrath are like rottenness of the bones," reads Proverbs 14:30 (AMPC).

Traci posted to social media: "My ninety-one-year-old grandmother got called for jury duty. At ninety-one, she's pretty judgmental, so she'd be tough on crime. At ninety-one, she's also not likely to remember what the case is about and just vote against whoever has hair hanging in their eyes."

Movies, cartoons, and comedy routines have been built on the concept of grumpy old men and grumpy old women. The audience laughs . . . unless the grumpy one, the embittered one, is Mom or Dad.

The adult child stands outside his parents' home, turns to his wife, takes a deep breath, and says, "Cover me. I'm going in." Into the war zone, the toxic battleground where old wounds remain infected long after infliction.

"Mom's bitterness over past hurts is destroying what may well be our final years together," Dan said. "With little else on which to focus these days, her anger over the way my father treated her has taken over as her reason for living. They divorced forty years ago. He's in a nursing home six states away. They haven't communicated since the day they signed the papers. But she never divorced herself from the resentment."

"Dad has something negative to say about every single

thing that happens in his day," Vince mourned. "He hates this. He hates that. If I visit him, I get blasted for not having visited sooner. His food is too hot or not hot enough. The room is too warm or too cold, and what are people doing, trying to upset him? That's his attitude. Mom has given up on him. She ignores it. I can't imagine living in that toxic atmosphere every day. If anything happens to Mom and Dad's only option is to move in with my wife and me, I may become a conscientious objector. I'm not a supporter of that war."

Few things are more beautiful than a man or woman of many years whose face is awash with peace and wisdom, softened by joy despite natural signs of aging. Few things are less attractive than an embittered old person.

"The ridiculous list of things my father finds to complain about would make a good comedy routine for television," said a son of a grumpy old man, "but it isn't funny to those of us who live with it."

Anger says "It's unfair" or "I can't control this"—two sentiments laced through many aging lives. The number of injustices, indignities, or decisions outside of an aging parent's control, the collection of the unfair, demeaning, confusing, or sad accelerates as age advances. Normal activities become pain-riddled, cumbersome, or laborious. Habits or hobbies that brought stress relief disappear.

It's natural that the unguarded mind would slip into

a pattern of focusing on past hurts or complaining about irritants. Natural, but not necessary. Understandable, but not inevitable.

When an infant fusses, a wise parent first investigates whether the distress is legitimate. Is the issue hunger? A wet diaper? Too hot? Too cold? A too-tight collar or a thread wrapped around a toe? Is the child crying out for reassurance of safety?

If the fussing continues, the young mom or dad tries to distract the child, change the environment—*Let's go for a walk*—or, as a last resort, let the child fuss it out. We're told that before the age of three—and some argue even later than that—a tactic of reasoning will fail almost a hundred percent of the time, since the part of the brain that allows for logic and reason is not yet developed.

As many of us age, the reasoning part of the brain retreats. Arguing with an aging parent to get them to stop arguing is futile. Trying to convince them that their bitterness is unfounded, wasted, or long expired may be met by bitterness of greater intensity. Heartbreaking as it is, without divine intervention, a long-held grudge will not "age out" of the system.

Proverbs 15:1 (isv) reminds us that "A gentle response diverts anger, but a harsh statement incites fury."

Veteran schoolteachers know that if they lower their voice to almost a whisper when the roomful of students has gotten out of control, they can reclaim quiet out of the chaos. Eventually, the students will calm and lean in to hear what the teacher is saying. The students' drive to not miss out on something others are hearing is stronger than their drive to continue feeding the chaos.

How does that work when people we care deeply about are the ones caught in a pattern of harsh words, criticism, a long-held grudge or resentment, or anger at the world?

- A soft answer
- A listening ear
- An attempt to understand their viewpoint
- God-fueled patience
- Diversionary tactics
- And when all else fails, let them fuss.

How do we maintain our own peace when our parents are locked in a self-made prison of unforgiveness or anger? Or when the diseases and ailments—even their treatment protocols—make them miserable and miserable to be near?

You may have worked hard to defuse your parents' anger, unsuccessfully. In the process, tension registered as knots in your neck muscles and a perpetual ache in your stomach. Peace has a chance when we refuse to be drawn into the fray, when we focus our attention on slow, steady breaths and on drawing our peace not from the atmosphere around us but from the unflappable, inexhaustible peace Christ gives. He doesn't dole out peace. He *is* our peace (Ephesians 2:14 ISV).

Ultimately, even in old age, our parents are to answer to God for their irritable attitude, not to us. And in this, as in a host of other issues related to loving an aging parent, prayer is not our last resort but, instead, our primary influencer for change.

"My mom was not a bitter woman," Tricia said, "despite all she endured, despite losing my sister to a homicide. The man who committed that crime was released near the time of my mother's last days. The rest of the family gritted our teeth and grumbled as the prisoner's time behind bars drew to an end. Mother told me, 'Tricia, I think it's time for me—for all of us—to let that go.'"

That kind of peace, the letting-go kind, comes through prayer and active faith.

Jesus, calm my parent's soul.
Wrap him, wrap her
In your swaddling embrace
Where the comfort is so strong
And the hold so secure
That they can't remember
The sting of irritants.
May they recall
How You answered their need
And forget
All but the warmth
Of Your love
And mine.

CHAPTER ELEVEN

When I Can't Let Old Hurts Go

Spend time in the hallway where nothing happens:
calming, preparing, growing, anticipating, repenting.

Taking care of my mom in her last days of lung cancer was difficult to the extreme," Vicki said. "She was not kind to me or my sisters while we were growing up. She did not have the ability to show love for us. Near the end of her life, she didn't ask much from us, either. But one evening she called us into the room and asked, 'Can you lie here with me?' My younger sister just could not do it and left the room.

"Somehow God gave me the grace to lie in the bed beside my mom," Vicki said, tears edging her voice. "Mom started stroking my hair. She told me how much she loved me. I lay beside her until she fell asleep. I crept out of the room and sobbed in the hallway for the precious gift God had just given me. My mom died a week later, and I knew she loved me. I might have missed it if I had let the painful memories dictate my behavior. Grace wins every time."

Around the world are adult children caring for aging parents they love. Or despise. Or fear. Or barely tolerate. Or adore and can't imagine living without. Some are caring for parents who harmed them physically, psychologically, emotionally, or sexually. The pain that riddles their caregiving tasks must seem unbearable.

A friend of mine is the primary caregiver for her elderly stepfather, a man who took advantage of her in her childhood. She takes him to his doctor appointments, cleans the wounds on his feet, cooks for him, cleans for him, and genuinely loves this man who repented years ago—not with words, but with his life. How is that possible?

My friend serves him with tears in her eyes over the way God has redeemed their relationship and erased the pain of the past. It isn't possible in all situations like theirs. But the work God did in forgiving him and healing her is unmistakable.

Darin's distance from his father was precipitated by a dramatic, memorable scene over Darin's choice of a life mate. They hadn't spoken to or seen each other for years when Darin received a call that would change everything. His father was no longer able to live on his own. Darin's aunt asked whether Darin and his wife would take him in. The natural response would have been to refuse. His father hadn't been there when Darin needed his support. He'd been hostile, angry, and unchanging in his vile attitude toward Darin's wife. Why should he—?

But Darin had learned firsthand how much damage angry, hurtful words could cause. He set aside his resentment and chose to serve his father with a generosity he wished he had received. Despite the time lost, their relationship was restored over the course of his father's decline because of Darin's humility and overt displays of selflessness. When his father died, both men were at peace.

"Will you love your father for My sake?" God seemed

to ask Darin. "Don't wait for him to deserve it or to apologize for how he treated you. Love him now. For Me."

"If possible, as far as it depends on you, live at peace with everyone," God said through the apostle Paul in Romans 12:18 (AMP). Reconciliation is high on His list of priorities.

We grow up with a mental picture of what love looks like—a picture influenced by nature, nurture, culture, and love fads (is love free or costly?). Our image of love is skewed by disappointment and twisted by heartbreak. It is warped by pop songs, Super Bowl commercials, and poorly written novels.

God says that love overlooks wrongs. Love forgives the petty—*He wouldn't let me extend my curfew on prom night*—and the huge—*She refused to come to my wedding.*

In 1 Corinthians 12, the apostle Paul ends the chapter by proposing that in our temporary, planned-obsolescent, listing, limping world, love is the preferred spiritual gift—freely available and universally applicable. Love rules the day, no matter what day it is. No matter what the challenge. No matter how deep the wounds.

A few verses later, he describes what godly love is like. We've heard those verses from 1 Corinthians 13 applied in sermons and wedding ceremonies. How would those familiar words read if applied to our relationships with aging parents?

Love for my aging parents is patient.

And, God, You know I need patience.

Love for my aging parents is kind.

I have to admit, Lord, that kindness is not always my default option.

Love for my aging parents isn't jealous.

Jealous? Not one of my issues. Or is it? Do I resent the attention they require? Where's the ME time?

It doesn't brag.

Stop my mouth, God, when pride gets in the way or makes me condescending.

It isn't arrogant.

Keep me, Lord, from acting as if their intelligence left just because their bodies are aging.

It isn't rude.

Lord, may it never be said of me that I disparaged my parents in public or otherwise.

It doesn't seek its own advantage.

Keep my motives pure, God.

Love for my aging parents isn't irritable.

It isn't? It shouldn't be. God, I need Your help with this one, too.

It doesn't keep a record of complaints.

My parents' nor my own. No record. New, blank slate every day.

It isn't happy about injustice, but it is happy with the truth.

I'd rather my parents maintain dignity than be proven wrong and me right.

Love for my aging parents puts up with all things . . .

All things.

Trusts in all things . . .

By Your Spirit, help me trust You to watch over my parents when I can't. And even when I can.

Hopes for all things . . .

Stir within me a hopeful attitude when I tiptoe too close to hopelessness as I watch them age.

Endures all things.

This temporary hardship, these few years of selflessness, Lord, I surrender to You.

Love for my aging parents never fails.

(Adapted from 1 Corinthians 13:3–8.)

The thirteenth chapter ends with the reminder that in life, three things remain: faith, hope, and love. The greatest of these, the most powerful, the most highly desired, the most influential, God says, is love.

Is your story one that serves as a testimonial to the power of love to overcome what once seemed unforgivable?

If I had the choice, Lord,
I'd hold on to
My well-deserved resentments
Until my dying day.

But the beauty of Your love
For me
Leaves me no
Viable
Option
Other than
Loving and forgiving.

Peace
Is too compelling
A prize.

CHAPTER TWELVE

When All We Can Do Is Laugh

To laugh in shadow of darkness
is its own source of light.

A home-hospice worker walked into my mother's apartment one day for a routine check and found my mom and me laughing together. "Hold on to your ability to laugh," she said, smiling. Then she sobered. "Those who lose their sense of humor have a harder time, no matter what the crisis. Aging included."

One of my mother's friends who later became a friend of mine tells about a day when that lesson hit home for her family. "Several years ago," she said, "my mom and grandma went on a day outing with several ladies from their church. Grandma was using a cane to get around, with my mom by her side.

"On the sidewalk ahead of us was a hopscotch pattern outlined in chalk. Grandma dropped her cane and shuffled through the whole hopscotch pattern, then picked up her cane and went on her way."

My friend said, "I think for a minute she became a little girl again. We could have scolded her, 'You'll break a hip!' Instead we laughed. It was good medicine, just like the Bible says."

Another friend, Valeri, still smiles over a story she often tells to illustrate her mother's sense of humor. "In spite of having had the part of her brain necessary for normal hearing and vision removed because of cancer, Mom had full fields of vision and normal hearing. Physically, she could walk and talk and soon started driving her car again (against doctor's orders, of course). She showed her surgeon that she could kick her legs as well as a cancan dancer, almost clipping his chin in her enthusiasm.

"'You can't take out just part of a Swede's brain,' Mother quipped. 'You have to take all of it out and hide it!'"

Mixed-up or missing words and names, car keys stored in odd places, mismatched socks, the inability to locate the car in a parking lot (due in part to the fact that Dad took the bus that day) . . . if we can't laugh about these incidents, we've missed the endorphins that help redeem those awkward moments.

Laughter *is* good medicine. When caring for our aging parents, letting them take the lead regarding humor may be key to maintaining the relationship. Parents laughed *at* will shrivel inside. But when laughter is mutual, shared, and comfortable for the parent, humor can serve as a face-saving grace.

A friend's father's aging process was accelerated by Parkinson's disease. The father's upbeat attitude set the tone for their family's survival. "Well, son," he said, "at least I don't have to stir my coffee anymore."

Undeveloped humor in either parent or child during younger years isn't likely to begin to sparkle with age. But humor that's grown tarnished from underuse can be polished to keep the aging process from becoming a rusty seriousness that drains the soul.

A close friend's experience illustrates the curiosity of commingled heartache and humor as parents age.

"My mom's been gone for eight years now," Wendy said, "but before she moved in with us, she lived in a little house about five miles away. Technology was always a challenge since she grew up in the era when a phone plugged into the wall and the television operated by a simple on/off knob and offered a mere handful of channels.

"I used to phone her often," my friend said, "just to keep in touch. I had been watching her grow somewhat frail as she moved into her eighties. It was always a blessing to share a quick call to see how she was and what she'd planned for her day. She'd often say, 'I'm going to be working in the garden this afternoon.' It became habitual for me to remind her to carry her portable phone so I could check in.

"One afternoon I couldn't reach her. I knew it was a gardening afternoon, so I thought she may have put the phone down and was working on a bed across the yard. I kept calling, at first every fifteen minutes or so. Then, picturing a fall, sunstroke, or worse, I called more frequently. Finally I got into the car to drive over and check on her.

"There she was in the garden, happily working on her topiary. 'Mom! Why didn't you answer your phone?' I had pictured a scenario that included an ambulance and the need to contact all my siblings.

"'My phone's right here. It never rang,' Mom said. In her hand was the television remote."

Wendy's mother had the grace to laugh off the incident, amused rather than frustrated by her mistake. Wendy treated it lightly. Because they could see the humor in the moment, it became a sweet addition to a vibrant garden of memories.

Their attitude had to have softened the transition when mother had to leave her garden and her home and move in with her caring, thoughtful, I-promise-to-laugh-with-you daughter.

In proper doses, at prescribed times, and at the invitation of the parent, laughter can serve a healing, relationship-bolstering role as our parents age. Tucked among all the serious admonitions and life lessons in God's Word is this one from Proverbs 17:22 (CEB): "A joyful heart helps healing, but a broken spirit dries up the bones."

Ane said, "Mama was in the last stages of Alzheimer's, and we'd flown to see her. I asked her if she liked my hair. She looked me in the eyes and said a flat, 'No.' I knew she had a moment of knowing exactly who I was.

"Mama hated it when I straightened my hair, and I had worn it straight that day. Her terse response was a gift from God. Three months later, she flew to heaven. While it may not sound tender to someone else, to me it was exactly what I needed."

"From the sidelines," Xochitl said, "I enjoyed my mom's giggles as she walked beside her girlfriends. Her eyes sparked with a joy and mischief I had never taken the time to notice before.

"Though I stumbled through my new role as her caregiver, I thanked God for the gift of watching my mom interact with others. For the first time in my life I got to know *Martha*, a woman with an interesting history, hobbies, and pet peeves. I grew to appreciate her as a sister in Christ who, like me, enjoyed music, dancing, lunch with friends, and laughter.

"Once I stopped focusing on the role my mother played, or was supposed to play, in my life, I discovered the treasure of knowing her as person. Martha was a beautiful, creative, loving, kind, compassionate, funny, and loyal sister, friend, neighbor, daughter, teacher, and wife. This brave woman was so much more than a mom."

In all our efforts to care for and encourage our aging parents, as we juggle prescription bottles and medical options and decision-making and safety features for their home, have we too often neglected the simple prescription of laughter? God calls it a healing remedy that is good, good medicine.

I wanted to keep you safe.
I forgot that laughter made you feel safe.
I wanted to keep you healthy.
I forgot that joy is better than adding
a medication.
I wanted you to feel comfortable.
But the pillow I bought did less than the
"Andy of Mayberry" rerun we shared.
I wanted to serve you, Mom and Dad.
You needed to tell your favorite joke. Again.
I wanted you to be happy.
The joy of the Lord is still our strength
(Nehemiah 8:10).

CHAPTER THIRTEEN

When My Parent Is in Denial

Denial isn't the enemy.
But it's no friend.

I remember the day when my mother was given the painful task of taking away Grandpa's keys. I'm sure she would say it was one of the most difficult assignments she'd faced . . . and she'd faced many.

She knew it would humiliate him and crush his spirit. His servant-heart had moved from hardworking farmer to church custodian to delivering meals among elderly shut-ins well into his eighties. Mom knew that telling him he could no longer drive would bring an end to what little freedom and independence he had left in his now ninety-year-old body. But it was a safety matter—for him and for others.

It had to be done. Mom tried to be as gentle as possible, as sensitive as she could be to what Grandpa would be feeling. But there's no easy way to say, "I'm taking away the keys."

Fast-forward several decades, and it was me and my siblings having that conversation with our mom. We hadn't noticed telltale but unmentioned scrapes down her vehicle, as Mom had Grandpa's. But we did see that Mom's responses had slowed to a dangerous level. Her heart was too weak to react quickly to anything, much less a road hazard. She'd self-limited her driving already. But when she talked with her version of logic that "If I die behind the wheel, I'll see Jesus sooner," we reminded her that other people's lives were at stake too, not hers alone.

As our parents age, we face a constant challenge to ensure they maintain their dignity, when so much of the aging process threatens to strip it away. God gave us a method to temper the moment when Mom had to face the reality that she would never—and *should* never—drive again. We appealed to her generous, giving, "how can I help?" heart.

"Mom, your car has been sitting idly in your garage for a long time now."

"Yes. I should just make the decision. I've always loved driving, you know. Love road trips. And maybe I'll be strong enough one of these days." She sighed and stared out the window as if an imaginary road trip were calling.

"Caleb and Amy have a car crisis." My daughter and son-in-law had started a used-car search with no success.

"They wouldn't want an old lady car." She dismissed the idea but then added, "Would they?"

Lord, help me to word this well. "It's a wonderful car. And you've taken good care of it. Would you like to talk to them about buying your car? Or renting it from you until you are ready to make a final decision?"

"If they can use it, . . ."

"It would be an answer to prayer for them."

Mom settled back in her chair. "I like being an answer to prayer."

"I know you do."

Denial and resistance follow parallel paths. Confrontation can merge the paths and form a tangled barricade. Misplaced optimism can throw a blockade in front of treatment or help.

"Aw, this pain in my jaw is nothing. I must have bit down too hard. I don't need to see a doctor."

"I can manage these steps. I just take it slow. Or I sit down and scoot myself backward up them. It takes a while, but I'm doing okay."

"So I missed a stop sign. Everyone misses a stop sign once in a while."

"I fell because the sidewalk was uneven. It's the city's fault. Yes, it's happening a lot lately. Why doesn't the city fix these sidewalks?"

"You'll never convince me to leave my home and go to one of those places. I'm doing fine here on my own. Just fine. There's nothing wrong with me that a little butting-out-of-my-business won't help."

"Dad, it's too much for you to handle anymore."

"I'm handling it. I'm . . . handling it."

God has been dealing with people living in denial since time began. He knows better than anyone how much denial can cost in lost opportunity, lost years, lost hope. In aging issues as in other areas, truth expressed with a sledgehammer may shock us into reality but do irreparable damage.

Truth expressed in love—there it is again—is what convinces us of our need for a Savior in Jesus. It's what holds us accountable to walk in ways that please Him. And truth expressed in love can also serve as the conduit for conversations with aging parents teetering between denial and resistance.

Reassurance of our love and support pave the way for times when it's necessary to confront with a reality check. Notice the word *necessary*.

As our parents age, logic and efficiency wrestle with concepts like kindness and does-it-really-matter? If he believes he's younger than he is, does it really matter? If she's convinced that her sister is still alive, what does it help to prove the hard truth? Will it change anything for the better?

On the other hand, if octogenarian Dad thinks he can still climb roofs and clean chimneys against doctor's orders—when his life or other lives are at stake—a reality check may be truly necessary.

If the fire department is called for the second time because Mom laid a dish towel across an open flame or Dad doesn't remember blacking out behind the wheel or Mom accidentally took an additional dose of her heart medication without realizing it, *necessary* takes precedence.

Love intervenes, but without pride, an "I told you so," or condescension. Love and respect working in tandem can minimize collateral damage when a parent camps on the banks of denial.

At two, I told you I could do it myself.
I couldn't.
I was in denial, but you loved me through it.

At five, I told you I didn't need your help
To ride without training wheels.
I was in denial, but you loved me through it.

At sixteen, I said I didn't need your advice
About dating.
I was in denial, but you loved me through it.

At twenty-two, I claimed I could figure out
My career path without your input,
Thank you very much.
I was in denial, but you loved me through it.

At thirty, I knew I could raise a child
Without your constant "Here's what you should do."
I was in denial, but you loved me through it.

And now you're aging.
And in denial.
It's an honor to love you through it.

CHAPTER FOURTEEN

When My Parent's Strongest Gift Is Stubbornness

Aging parents want dignity and usefulness.
Grown children want to know that their parents are happy,
well cared for, content, and at peace. Can those goals coexist?

Is stubbornness a spiritual gift? Tenacity, maybe. Perseverance. But as our parents age, we tend to view tenacity as stubbornness.

A Bible-study friend said, "My father-in-law stopped at Burger King on the way to the hospital while having a heart attack because they wouldn't have good food in the emergency room. Can you imagine?"

I could have countered with the story of my sixty-two-year-old mother who, while staying three hours away with an old friend from nursing school, woke with symptoms she knew signaled a heart attack. Instead of telling her hostess, she packed up and drove the three hours home—because she wanted "her own" hospital.

"My father wrapped his belt around his thigh, above the bone sticking out of his leg, and finished planting corn before he agreed that an ambulance might be a good idea," said another friend.

Elizabeth says, "My mother tried her hardest to wrap presents for Christmas. It took her forever to get the job done. She had always done the wrapping alone and with great efficiency. But dementia had taken away the ability to do this simple task. She couldn't even zip off a simple piece of tape. I watched her and mourned. I mourned for her memory loss and confusion but also grieved that in all likelihood, I would no longer receive a wrapped present from my mom. Watching her frustration caused me great pain on so many levels. Yet she insisted on trying."

My husband tells me that when the time comes for his headstone to be carved, he wants the sentiment to mimic one he heard long ago: "See? I told you I was sick." He's trying to get me to promise I'll follow through with that. But I can be tenacious too.

Stubborn can be cute, cutting, or potentially catastrophic, as with a delayed ambulance. Stubborn and dangerous share more than a little common ground. But if we examine the issue closely, much of what we determine to be ornery stubbornness in our aging parents is a tango of two persistent, persevering people: the parent and us.

I adopted one true story of a new perspective on the tango for a novel written a few years ago. A nursing-home resident refused to take her medication on the morning shift. The more the nurse insisted, the harder the older woman pressed her lips together and turned her head to the side into her pillow.

The battle raged until another nurse took the time to ask the resident why she consistently refused to take her morning medicine.

"That nurse gives me ice water to take my pills. I have all my own teeth, and I'm proud of it. But they're sensitive to cold. I've told her that, but she won't change her routine with the ice water."

"You'd stop fussing about it if she brought you luke-warm water?"

"Of course. I'm old; I'm not stupid."

What are we insisting on that makes our parent look like the stubborn one in the relationship? Some gerontology experts advise, "If it isn't dangerous to their health or some-one else's, against the law, or emotionally risky, let it go."

Philippians 2:3–4 (ESV) speaks to those who don't want their own stubborn streak to get in the way of caring for and honoring their aging parents: "Do nothing from self-ish ambition or conceit, but in humility count others more significant than yourselves. Let each of you look not only to his own interests, but also to the interests of others."

Meeting my widowed mother's needs during the last years of her life wasn't always convenient. But none of us are called to convenience—we're called to serve others. Most of the time, love propelled my actions. On occasion, a time crunch or responsibility overload smudged my good intentions.

Confined to bed, my mother had few options for en-tertainment other than Gaither music and recordings of her sister's trio, which played nonstop in her room. Reading ex-hausted her. Her eyes couldn't focus on the television screen for long. Even her Bible reading had to be in short spurts. But she could play Solitaire on a small handheld electronic game unit.

One day, the game's batteries died. It caused her an inordinate amount of frustration that she had no extra batteries. I lived a half hour away but promised that I would pick up new batteries the next time I was in town. That wasn't good enough. Mom called my sister who lived in town, but she was in a daylong meeting at work. She, too, promised to get new batteries as soon as possible, but the earliest she could do it would be too late in the day to take them to Mom's room at the hospice residence.

Mom's agitation seemed far out of proportion to the problem. When she called me a second time, I was on the verge of saying, "Mother. It's Solitaire. A game. You can be a little patient." Instead, I rearranged my schedule and made a trip into town.

During a recent recovery from a minor medical procedure, I discovered an online game that helped me pass the time and challenged my brain's agility. While I couldn't read for long stretches and or sit at my computer to work, I could stave off boredom with a few rounds of the game.

Only then, six years after Mom's meltdown over batteries, did I realize that her inability to have that small need met was a far bigger issue to her than it was to any of the rest of us. She had little else. When it wasn't available to her, the loss was magnified by how few options she had. I'd thought her impatient and demanding. Instead, she was hurting.

Mom also insisted on having a fan blowing, no matter the season or the temperature in the room. When she finally confessed that the moving air helped her weary lungs breathe, our irritation and the chill we felt with that noise and air blowing all the time abated. We learned to wear a sweater or wrap in a blanket so she could breathe.

It was a solemn, love-hemmed moment when, a few minutes after her passing, we turned off the fan. The whirring sound we'd listened to during the years of her illness turned to silence. She no longer needed the fan to breathe because Jesus was breathing for her.

We missed the sound, the awkward and at-times-interfering breeze. But we didn't regret having listened when we thought she was just being stubborn.

Father God, help me celebrate
The tenacity
That made my parents
Survivors,
The perseverance
They passed on
To me.
Guide me
To use it well,
In ways that
Respect my heritage
And honor You.

CHAPTER FIFTEEN

When My Parents Make Unwise Decisions

If we didn't care, it wouldn't hurt so much.
If we didn't care, how shallow life would be.

Is Christina's story yours? She said, "The hardest part of my father's aging is putting aside my deep ache from his choices over the last few years. After my stepmother died, he met a woman, walked away from me and my family, and acted as if we'd never mattered. Now he has Parkinson's disease, and each time I see him, I have to fight to let the hurt go and just love him where he is."

"My father," another friend said, "married weeks after Mom died. We understood his loneliness, but how could that not seem disrespectful to Mom's memory? The new woman freely admitted she didn't love Dad. She wanted his money. Which she took. Dad was so desperate for companionship, he didn't care."

How aging parents invest their money, their time, and their affections matter to us because we care about their future—however long or short—and their health and happiness. If we didn't care, it wouldn't hurt when the decisions they make seem unwise or downright foolish.

Seemingly obvious scams may not be as obvious to a generation that assumed people were, for the most part, trustworthy and that their investments were safe, their information private, their personal details nobody else's business.

Christina's father fell for a relationship trap—one that convinced him that leaving his family was a fair exchange for companionship with a woman.

Others fall for a looks-so-good-on-the-surface financial scheme or succumb to the fear of reporting abuses and neglect. They avoid "bothering" their doctors or withhold information from their caregiver children because they "don't want to worry them."

We can inform our aging parents. We can advocate for them, defend them, represent them. We can intervene when necessary. We can assume responsibility with power of attorney or financial power of attorney status to keep our parents from potentially devastating decisions.

A healthy parent-child relationship establishes a level of trust that comes into play when our parents' decision-making abilities falter. And a foundation of love well demonstrated in the past may ease tensions when the present is threatened by unwise decisions. "Dad, I can't let you do that." "Mom, I know you don't see the harm in stopping that medicine without consulting your doctor. So I'm asking you to talk to him about it for my peace of mind. And if you don't call him, because I love you, I will."

No human is equipped or able to protect another human flawlessly, however. We can't be ever-present or all-knowing, always understanding what's happening inside our parents' minds and hearts. Neither can we always be aware of others' motives.

Omniscient. Omnipresent. Omnipotent.

God.

We entrust our parents into God's care as we do our children when we leave them in the church nursery, send them off to kindergarten, let them stay overnight with a friend, leave them at the college dorm, or give our blessing to their marriage. We can't be with them all the time or observe every threat against them.

But God can. He sees what we can't, and as Psalm 91:4 says, He shelters those who trust Him in the shadow of His wings. His promises are many.

"The eyes of the Lord are in every place, keeping watch on the evil and the good" (Proverbs 15:3 ESV).

"Great is our Lord, and abundant in power; his understanding is beyond measure" (Psalm 147:5 ESV).

He declares "the end from the beginning and from ancient times things not yet done, saying, 'My counsel shall stand, and I will accomplish all my purpose,'" (Isaiah 46:10 ESV).

Consider Psalm 139:1–4 (ESV) with your parents' names inserted for the word *me*:

O LORD, you have searched [my parents] and known [them]! You know when [they] sit down and when [they] rise up; you discern [their] thoughts from afar. You searched out [their] path and [their] lying down and are acquainted with all [their] ways. Even before a word is on [their] tongue, O LORD, you know it altogether.

When collecting my thoughts—and His—regarding the book in your hands, I wondered at first how many verses in the Bible applied directly to the topic of aging parents. I could count on one hand the passages that seemed like givens:

"Honor your father and mother" (Exodus 20:12; Ephesians 6:2).

"Religion that God our Father accepts as pure and faultless is this: to look after orphans and widows in their distress and to keep oneself from being polluted by the world" (James 1:27 NIV).

"Even when I am old and gray, do not forsake me, my God, till I declare your power to the next generation, your mighty acts to all who are to come" (Psalm 71:18 NIV).

"[Growing in grace] they will still thrive and bear fruit and prosper in old age; they will flourish and be vital and fresh [rich in trust and love and contentment]" (Psalm 92:14 AMP).

"If anyone fails to provide for his own, and especially for those of his own family, he has denied the faith [by disregarding its precepts] and is worse than an unbeliever [who fulfills his obligation in these matters]" (1 Timothy 5:8 AMP).

But as I turned the revered pages of my Bible, I discovered that—as with any subject of concern to humanity—it *all* held practical application and encouragement. The words are infused with the Spirit of the Living God, the Omniscient One, the One who not only cares but equips *us* to care well, the One who simultaneously holds those we love and us.

This Book—God's Word—is the caregiver's primary survival resource. If opening up the pages does nothing more than mentally and spiritually reconnect us to our source of help, then it has served a holy purpose in that moment. But His Word does so much more.

It answers the questions that nag even the faith-filled as our parents age:

- Who will watch over my parents when I can't be there?
- Who can comfort his/her anxiety when nothing seems to work?
- Who can bring peace into this situation?
- Who can redeem this crisis we're in?

- Who can calm, heal, and deliver?
- Where will my parents and I find hope in this tender but trying season?

In some families, the word *impossible* laces many conversations. "Dad is being impossible!" "Finding a safe place for Mom to live right now is impossible." "Dealing with the insurance company/medical team/rest of the family is impossible." "It's impossible to get the answers we need regarding my parent's condition." "The choices Dad and Mom are making frighten me, but they won't listen. What am I going to do? I don't want to see them hurt or taken advantage of. It's impossible."

The pages of our Bibles rustle as we turn them, searching for hope. We find it in Matthew 19:26 (NLT) where we read, "Jesus looked at them intently and said, 'Humanly speaking, it is impossible. But with God everything is possible.'"

Jesus, turn Your gaze to me
Look at me intently
And speak Your words of comfort
Over me
And my aging parents.

Jesus, turn Your gaze to me
Look at me intently
And calm my troubled heart
That cares as it should
But carries what You volunteered to bear.

Jesus, turn Your gaze to me
Look at me intently
And I in turn
Will look to You
In this season
And always.

Rock of Aging, cleft for me,
Let me hide myself in Thee.

CHAPTER SIXTEEN

When My Gratitude Gets Lost in Life's Wrinkles

How far back would you have to trace
to find something to be grateful for?
Make the journey.

The home into which Pam was born was a hostile, dangerous place for a child. For anyone. Poisoned by alcoholism and abuse, it spelled *home* with different letters: F–E–A–R.

She's grateful to have survived those beginnings. She's grateful God redeemed those years of torment and gave her a godly husband, God-serving children and grandchildren, and a ministry to others enriched by the restoration she's experienced.

In a video conversation the other day, she said, "I'm grateful for something else that I didn't think about until now. When my dad was at his worst—violent and out of control—my mom would tell us kids, 'Get your shoes on. We're going for a walk.' Early in my life, that established a pattern of turning to exercise rather than to negative influences to cope with trauma. I wouldn't have thought to thank God for that gift born in the middle of such a horrific home life."

The heavyheartedness of watching loving parents age. The ache of watching unloving parents near the end of an opportunity for reconciliation. Knowing the pain our parents experience has intensified. The natural weariness of caregiving. When they become too much to bear, how far back would we need to trace, how deeply would we have to probe to find something for which to be grateful?

Gabrielle relates a story of finding a priceless jewel of gratitude in her grandfather's story. Her grandpa Art had had a brain aneurysm when she was three, so she never knew him the way other people did. Partially blind and walking with a cane, sometimes he knew who she was and sometimes he didn't. He lived that way for twenty-seven years.

In 2009, when Gabrielle was a young mom, her grandfather was diagnosed with pancreatic cancer. It quickly overcame what little ability and energy he had left. His nine children assembled from all over the country. A bed was set up in the TV room, where Gabrielle's grandparents slept together for the last few weeks of his life.

"One evening," Gabrielle says, "my mom and dad picked me up at my house to take me to see my grandparents. Dad turned on the tape player in his truck and I heard a voice that sounded strangely familiar—but also strangely unfamiliar. It was my grandfather as a younger man, giving his testimony shortly after he'd committed his life to Christ. I cried as I listened to him speak of the grace and forgiveness of God and the ultimate sacrifice of His one and only Son.

"I cried," she said, "not only because of the depth of emotion, but also because I never really knew the man speaking the words. When we arrived at my grandparents' house, we stayed in the truck to finish the tape. After it ended, my mom said, 'Did you know it was Grandpa who introduced all of us to Christ?'

"I was in awe that I had never heard the story or realized how he had impacted the faith journey so many of us had taken. Grandpa had welcomed Christ into our family and led the way for me to know Him too. I was overcome with the knowledge and suddenly needed to thank him before it was too late. I also realized I had never told my grandpa I loved him.

"When we walked into the house, several aunts and uncles were gathered in the kitchen, speaking in low tones. They said Grandma had just gone to bed but I could go in and say hi. I walked around the makeshift curtain between the living room and TV room. What I saw brought more tears to my eyes. My grandma, who had faithfully cared for my grandpa all those years, was snuggled up behind him with her arms wrapped around his waist. Grandpa was sleeping, but my grandma was still awake. She gave me a beautiful, sad smile. I didn't want to wake my grandpa, so I simply placed a kiss on his cheek and told him I loved him, and then I whispered 'Thank you.' It was the last time I saw him on this side of heaven."

When gratitude gets lost in sadness, routine, responsibility, harsh memories, pregrieving, or the indignities of current reality, it's worth the journey to trace back to where we last sensed gratitude's presence.

Gratitude for who our parents are or who they were buoys us when caregiving grows tiresome. Gratitude for having survived rough seas keeps us dipping our paddles into the water to move forward. Gratitude for small things, tiny details—like Pam's exercise habit—soothes us like cool air on a sweltering evening.

A heart of gratitude may need to be cultivated if it doesn't spring up naturally. Gratitude is a little like friendship bread. When it's used often, it grows to provide more—an endless supply. Enough to share with the whole neighborhood.

We want a clear answer to the question, "God, how do You want me to handle this stage of life as my parents age?" His answer is to find reason to give thanks, even now. "Give thanks in all circumstances; for this is the will of God in Christ Jesus for you" (1 Thessalonians 5:18 esv).

"And whatever you do, in word or deed, do everything in the name of the Lord Jesus, giving thanks to God the Father through him" (Colossians 3:17 esv).

"*Whatever,* Lord? Even—?"

Yes. Even that.

"Therefore let us be grateful for receiving a kingdom that cannot be shaken, and thus let us offer to God acceptable worship, with reverence and awe" (Hebrews 12:28 ESV).

"My parents' footsteps are growing shaky. Their hands tremble too much to hold a pen anymore."

Let's be grateful for the kingdom that can't be shaken, for their future in heaven where nothing will be shaky or shaken and the only trembling will stem from awe.

"And let the peace of Christ rule in your hearts, to which indeed you were called in one body. And be thankful" (Colossians 3:15 ESV).

"Peace and gratitude in tandem, Lord?"

Yes.

Help me, God, to see this season
As a season of thanksgiving.
Grow my gratitude
To full maturity,
A ripe harvest
Of thankfulness.
And show me ways
To express it
So my parents are blessed
And You retain the glory.

CHAPTER SEVENTEEN

When I Don't Know What to Pray

*Not knowing how to respond when
our parents are in pain
or their memory fades or disappears
is more a sign of our loving devotion
than it is our inadequacy. Take heart.*

His sagging slippers hung over the end of the footrest as he sat in his recliner, watching a documentary about a hijacker who had called himself Dan Cooper. More than forty years ago, the mystery man had commandeered a plane and asked for $200,000 in twenty-dollar bills and four parachutes.

The father sat a little straighter in his recliner and asked, "What would a hijacker want with four pair of shoes?"

It was the kind of statement that makes offspring wonder whether Dad needs hearing aids or if his mind is slipping. Or was it a simple misunderstanding? (*Thank you, beloved husband of mine, for allowing me to use this example of a simple misunderstanding.*)

As we notice signs of aging in our parents, we often find ourselves wondering, "Is this something I should be worried about?"

- He seems unsteady on his feet.
- She's falling more often.
- He's missing the ends of sentences.
- She drifts off in the middle of conversations.
- He complains that the light is too dim when it's fine for everyone else in the room.
- She can't remember names.
- He can't remember dates.
- She didn't hear her grandchild say "I love you."

How much is part of the natural aging process—unpleasant but not disconcerting—and how much of it is symptomatic of something more serious?

Do I step in or stay out of it? Do I force the issue or wait until my parent has a major incident and then regret not having spoken up?

God's Word gives us a clear indication of an answer to one of the above questions—*Should I be worried?*

Philippians 4:6 tells us, "Don't be worried about anything; instead, pray about everything; tell God your needs, and don't forget to thank him for his answers." That's how I memorized it from the Living Bible paraphrase.

The New International Version expresses it this way: "Do not be anxious about anything, but in every situation, by prayer and petition, with thanksgiving, present your requests to God."

Would God want us to make an exception to the "Don't be worried; don't be anxious" instruction when it comes to concerns about our aging parents?

"Don't be worried about *anything*."

How are we supposed to comply with that directive when love for our parents makes it natural to worry?

"Instead, pray about *everything*. In *every* situation, by prayer and petition, with thanksgiving, present your requests to God" (mashup of both versions).

What a courage-building invitation to pray about

everything. God not only allows but invites us to present our requests before Him. The word *everything* encompasses even those oh-so-automatic worrisome issues with our parents.

Our intelligence, research, powers of observation, and powers of persuasion only go so far in assessing and reacting to our parents' needs.

"Pray," God says.

"About what?"

"Everything."

"God, I . . . I think she might need Miralax. I can't pray about—"

"Even that."

When in doubt about how to pray for our parents, we can turn to the prayers recorded for us in the Bible. Many are easily adaptable to our parents' needs or anxieties. It's as easy as reading a verse then praying in your own words.

Ephesians 1:18–19 (NIV): "I pray that the eyes of your heart may be enlightened in order that you may know the hope to which he has called you, the riches of his glorious inheritance in his holy people, and his incomparably great power for us who believe."

Yes, God. Please fill my parents' minds and hearts with thoughts about what awaits them and how quickly You will erase from their memories anything of this earth that brought them pain.

Romans 15:13 (NIV): "May the God of hope fill you with all joy and peace as you trust in him, so that you may overflow with hope by the power of the Holy Spirit."

Father God, flood my parents with hope, joy, faith, and peace. May those gifts grow and multiply within them as they inch toward heaven.

Third John 1:2 (ESV): "Beloved, I pray that all may go well with you and that you may be in good health, as it goes well with your soul."

Lord, I spend so much time in prayer for their health needs. Keep me faithful to pray for the needs of their souls.

Philippians 4:19 (NIV): "And [I pray that] my God will meet all your needs according to the riches of his glory in Christ Jesus."

I know about many of their needs, Father God. But You know them even better. I pray that not one will escape Your notice or mine as together we minister to them.

We have the ability to apply personal stress relief—freedom from worry—and to bless our parents with the same act—praying for them. The by-product is peace. And His peace is not hampered by barricades of mental confusion.

Many stories are told of elderly parents who had lost their ability to tell left from right and could remember nothing they'd heard moments ago, but who prayed with crisp and heartfelt clarity or could recall all the words of all the verses of their favorite hymns. When talking to God, their impairment didn't get in the way.

Verse seven of Philippians 4 (NIV) tells us that after we have prayed and thanked God for His answers on the way, "the peace of God, which transcends all understanding, will guard your hearts and your minds in Christ Jesus."

Imagine God's peace encircling us while we navigate these uncertain waters. Inexpressible comfort lies within that promise.

Ageless One,
I never knew
That aspect
Of Your character
Would hold
So much
Comfort.

You,
Ageless One,
Unchanging One,
Be for my parents
All that they
Need,
All they're missing,
All they've lost.

And the same
For me.
Amen.

CHAPTER EIGHTEEN

When My Parent's Mind Is Gone

A familiar college promotion from a few years back—
"A mind is a terrible thing to waste."
A familiar cry when the issue is dementia or Alzheimer's—
"A mind wasting away is a terrible thing to watch."

Heartbreaking.

That's how many describe a dementia diagnosis. A cancer diagnosis is frightening, yet loaded with hope that medication, radiation, surgery, or a combo platter can bring remission or a cure and a return to normal life.

The words *dementia* and *Alzheimer's* hold no such hope, as of this writing. When mental function decays or begins its descent, few options remain but to adjust and trust, and to cope and cry when we have to.

Heartbreaking.

"As Mom started to lose her mental awareness of the here-and-now, she became so sure of what she thought she saw and heard," my friend Karen said. "She lived in a suite in the lower level of our home. Late one night I noticed her door wide open, the TV blaring, and all the lights on. When I went downstairs to investigate, she said, 'Oh boy, do I have something to tell you!'

"She said a movie-production company had come into the house and moved out all my furniture and then all her furniture and filmed a movie. She was so surprised I had not heard all the noise they'd made. I tried to assure her that there was no way they would come into our home without permission, nor would they do it while I slept upstairs. I showed her how the furniture was all in place and no lights were on in any other part of the house except for her apartment. She was so sure, arguing vehemently that she'd been in the middle of a movie a few minutes earlier. I argued more. Finally, she sat in her big rocker, folded her arms and said, 'Well! We will just have to agree to disagree.'

"I'm not sure what lesson that teaches," Karen said, "except that now I realize I shouldn't have argued."

Elizabeth mourned the loss of her mother's consistency. Once a sweet-tempered, innocent woman with a wide heart, her temperament changed at dementia's hands. "A nurse from the assisted-living center called one night to tell me that my mother had been hitting people. My mother. I was asked to come to the center to see if I could calm her down.

"When I arrived," Elizabeth told me, "my mother was sitting at a table, quietly eating a granola bar. I sat beside her and asked if she was okay. She nodded and smiled. I then asked her whether she had hit anyone. She looked astonished and said, 'Of course not!'

"Without missing a beat, she leaned toward me and whispered, 'But I kicked a few.'

"'Mom, you can't do that.' She would have been mortified if she'd been aware of what she was doing and saying.

"'I will if they need it,' she said, and she quietly went back to eating her granola bar."

Listening to that story as outsiders, we can catch the

bits of humor in the incident. We cling to those moments during a season when humor provides much-needed respite from so much heartbreak.

"My father always had so many interests—antiques, machinery, beautiful things, politics, TV, reading, my children," Vickie said. "I loved buying gifts for my dad because I knew what he would enjoy. He would go on and on if he really liked the gift. Then he got very sick and had *no* interests. Nothing could get his attention. In my Christmas card to family and friends that year, I wrote that all interests had left him . . . and then he left us for a better life."

Fragile minds.

One of God's greatest mercies is His compassion for the fact that we are frail, fragile, vulnerable. He knows we are *like dust*, the Bible tells us. So He pours all the more loving-kindness and compassion on us, even when—or especially when—our minds are fragile.

I had not seen my aunt for a couple of years and had no idea how tight a grip dementia had taken. Always a strong woman before, she appeared frail and uncertain of everything—her footsteps, where to train her eyes to look at the people in the room, the proper protocol for welcoming guests. . . .

I took the paper cup she offered me, not at all certain I should have let her get me something to drink. Where had she gotten the water? It may have been curious of me to wonder, but it wasn't unreasonable. The cup she handed me with a wide smile had a half-moon of red lipstick on its rim. Had Aunt Gladys taken a sip of it herself? No. She wasn't wearing lipstick. From what long-forgotten party had the paper cup been saved? And what was I supposed to do now?

Aunt Gladys had insisted on serving me something to drink. I'd thought a glass of water a safe choice, considering the contorted paths her mind often took those days. I didn't want to offend or agitate her. Was it time to pray, "Lord, cover me" and take a sip?

Dr. Gauri Khatkhate, geriatric psychiatrist with Chicago's Loyola University Stritch School of Medicine and the Edward Hines Jr. VA Hospital advises that when dementia affects a family, our strength lies in arming ourselves with understanding. "Recognize that your loved one now exists in a confusing and frightening world," says Khatkhate.

"Your mom or dad may lack a good way of expressing physical or emotional discomfort," Khatkhate observes. "Instead, they may seem to lash out in anger—shouting, insults, cursing, or physical aggression. Those are not genuine thoughts or feelings; they are the symptoms of a devastating disease. Recognizing and understanding that fact may help lessen the emotional impact of the behavior."

Good counsel.

But we might wonder if God had children of Alzheimer's patients in mind when He wrote through the psalmist, "He heals the brokenhearted and binds up their wounds" (Psalm 147:3 NIV).

Lord, hear my prayer.

I miss my mom's cooking
Gone, now that the letters
On the recipe card
Make no sense to her
Anymore.

I miss my father's laughter
And the corny jokes
He no longer tells
Because he can't remember
The punchline
Or the first line either.

I miss the joy on my parents' faces
When I come home for the holidays.
They still smile,
But I'm not sure
They know who I am
Or how much they mean
To me.

CHAPTER NINETEEN

When I Think I Can't
Make an Impact

God will take you to Plan Z and then say,
"Where's the rest of your alphabet?"

—Author unknown

We can't halt or even slow the aging process for our parents or grandparents.

I paused after writing those words. They stood so starkly against the white of the computer-page background.

We can't stop this from happening.

But that doesn't mean we are helpless to make an impact on these years and our loved ones' comfort. A wise, studied, informed, compassionate child is a gift to an aging parent, no matter what diseases or disorders complicate the scene.

As my mother aged and I attempted to meet her physical and emotional needs, a single sentence replayed in my mind: *How would I want to be treated if I were the aging mother and my daughter or sons were caring for me?*

Rachael Wonderlin, who has a masters' degree in gerontology, considered the same question when she wrote "16 Things I Would Want if I Got Dementia" (alzheimersreadingroom.com; July 30, 2016). It is easy to see how her points would matter to an aging parent even if dementia were not an issue. Briefly, she says:

- I would want friends and family to embrace my reality. Let me believe whatever I believe.
- Talk to me like an adult, not a child.
- Take the time to figure out why I'm agitated.
- Treat me the way you would want to be treated.

- Don't talk about me as if I'm not in the room.
- Don't feel guilty if you cannot care for me 24/7.
- Don't act frustrated if I mix up names, events, or places.
- Don't exclude me from parties and family gatherings.
- Know that I still like hugs and handshakes.
- Remember that I am still the person you know and love.

The Alzheimer's Care Resource Center in Florida adds some guidelines for keeping relationships in good repair when parents are well into the aging process or battling dementia. This counsel aligns with the growing but hard-to-swallow wisdom that tells us to avoid correcting what we see as "mistakes" in our aging parents. It won't help to try to correct them if their minds aren't functioning as they once did and logic is no longer strong. It won't make a difference later. In the long run, it doesn't matter. But the attempt at correction is certain to add to the parent's level of frustration—and the caregiver's as well.

In its "Alzheimer's Communication" poster, the Resource Center says:

- Never argue. Instead, agree.
- Never reason. Instead, divert.

- Never shame. Instead, distract.
- Never lecture. Instead, reassure.
- Never say, "Remember?" Instead, reminisce.
- Never say, "I told you." Instead, repeat and regroup.
- Never say, "You can't." Instead, let them do what they can.
- Never condescend. Instead, encourage.

Note how many of those points coincide with what God advises in His Word.

"Love covers a multitude of sins," says 1 Peter 4:8 (NLT).

"Above all, have fervent and unfailing love for one another, because love covers a multitude of sins [it overlooks unkindness and unselfishly seeks the best for others]" (1 Peter 4:8 AMP).

"Be kind, compassionate, and forgiving to each other, in the same way God forgave you in Christ" (Ephesians 4:32 CEB).

"The anger of man does not produce the righteousness of God" (James 1:20 ESV).

What other practical ideas will help us love our aging parents well, even when dementia gets in the way—as it will for one in nine Americans over age sixty-five and one-third of Americans over the age of eighty-five, according to the Alzheimer's Association?

"My dad was a hunter, a fisherman, and a trapper," Sheila says. "That's where his heart was. When he was overcome with cancer, he was in the hospital way down at the end of the wing. We visited him regularly, but there were times when no one could be there with him. So we bought him a CD of lake sounds.

"He was hard of hearing from working in the mill. One day we got off the elevator in the middle of the floor and heard lake loons, as clear as anything. It didn't dawn on us until we started walking that the loons were coming from Dad's room. He had turned up the CD so he could hear it. He'd always had a great sense of humor, but this time he was not trying to be funny. A little loony, maybe."

Another friend of mine said, "One of my brothers brought a painting of an elderly man praying at the dining table to the assisted-living center so Mom would see something familiar when she opened her eyes. We filled her room with cards and plants and family."

"We tapped into what Dad could remember," yet another friend told me. "He couldn't recall what year it was or his own age, but he remembered every word of his favorite songs from the 1940s. So we kept that music playing in his room. It calmed him and lit his eyes with recognition that only kicked in when the music played."

"Music imprints itself in the brain deeper than any other human experience. . . . Music brings back the feeling of life when nothing else can," observed neurologist Dr. Oliver Sacks.

Carrie tells how the gift of music eased the emotional pain of watching her grandmother approaching her final days. "One day we were sitting with her while she was getting anxious. My mom (her daughter) suggested we sing some hymns. No matter what Alzheimer's took away from my Sunday-school-teacher grandmother, it couldn't take away 'Jesus Loves Me.' Grandmother sang every word— with gusto.

"At the end, as we sang the final notes of the Bible tells me so, she added 'PERIOD.' Emphatically. Such a tender touch from God for all of us.

"We even sang 'Jesus Loves Me' at her funeral. Our music minister made sure we all added 'PERIOD' at the end."

Creator God,
For whom inventing worms that make silk
And bee regurgitation that becomes sweet honey
And foxgloves that
Provide medicine
That regulates
A human heartbeat
Were no great challenge,
Feed me ideas
Daily
For how I can make a difference
In my parents' lives.

CHAPTER TWENTY

When My Parent Loses Who I Am

The four saddest words:
"She doesn't remember me."

Our parents' aging can start small . . . or catastrophically. I lingered over two separate but equally sobering social-media posts the other day. One said, "Three of the saddest words I've ever written: my mother was." The writer had returned from the funeral that necessitated the verb change from "my mother is" to "my mother was."

The second post sounded similar, initially. "My four saddest words: She doesn't remember me."

As our parents age, we can find reasons to laugh together over forgetting a phone number or a shirt put on backward or mismatched shoes or having to walk more slowly "so Dad can keep up." But when aging is twisted and distorted by dementia, we're hollowed by the impenetrable wall it erects. How can a parent/child relationship do anything but crumble when dementia gets in the way? How can a mother forget her own child?

We expect the connection between a parent and child to be a loving one that does not end. But for too many of us, dementia gets in the way of parental love. It can even steal our parents' or grandparents' recognition of who we are and that we mattered to them.

What drives us to want to correct what a dementia patient gets "wrong"? Our incessant, relentless need to be right? Our underlying belief that if we choose the perfect word picture or repeat our point often enough, we'll break through the hardened cement that keeps the wall in place?

It's been proven futile. Our intellect knows it's futile. Yet we persist. Especially when the memory that's missing is who we are, our identity.

"If I tell the right story or remind her of an experience we shared together or ground her in reality, she'll remember who I am to her."

"If I find that one elusive piece to his mental puzzle, it'll come flooding back to him that I'm his son. He's my father. We've been each other's best friend for forty years."

But our efforts result in frustration, not breakthroughs.

Could God be calling us to step onto their playground for a while rather than drag them into the so-called real world? Our real world is a game for which they've lost the pieces, the rule book, and all the history of past wins and losses.

Imagine being invited to participate in a game where the instructions are in a foreign language, a language everyone in the room knows except for you. Imagine being chided for missing your turn when you didn't even know the game had started. Picture how overwhelmed and lost you would feel when everyone else acted as if the game were a matter of life and death.

We find it no great leap to sit at a small table with a grandchild, throw pink boas around our necks, and sip imaginary tea from tiny plastic teacups with our pinkies raised as high as our pretend British accents. Why would we insist on fighting for an impossible reality with our parents or grandparents as they age?

If Mom needs to nap before her ballet recital, what purpose is served by telling her it's a ridiculous notion?

If Dad insists he won a golf tournament the day before, although he hasn't left the assisted-living facility in two years, who are we to insist that he didn't? And what purpose does it serve?

By contrast, how high a purpose is served when we risk stepping into their reality for a while?

We who still have our faculties could be the first to celebrate, helping Dad slip into the green suit jacket we found at the secondhand store and making room on the shelf for the trophy he'll forget should be coming in the mail any day now.

When my sister-in-law's twins were born, she covered the wall above their changing table with family photos. No family members lived close by. My sister-in-law was determined to help her girls gain an infant's sense that the face was familiar when grandmas and grandpas or aunts and uncles came to visit.

Before the twins could talk, they'd memorized those faces.

Sometimes, a wall of family photos will help an Alzheimer's patient gain a flash of recognition, even if the name doesn't accompany it. But in other cases, the sea of faces is like a kindergartener's version of a Picasso, distorted and hard to explain.

Elaine never knew in which era her father was residing when she checked on him in the mornings during the months he lived with her. "One day, he was spying for the government during the war. Pick a war. Any war. The next day, he thought his bed was a raft and he was adrift on a doldrummed sea. 'Save yourself!' he'd say, tossing me a pillow life preserver. The next day, he'd be tapping out a rhythm on his nightstand, claiming to be practicing for Carnegie Hall.

"As out of touch as he was with reality," Elaine said, "life was far from boring. I decoded secret messages for him, spent an hour 'treading water' while I cleaned his room, and applauded wildly when he finished practicing for his concert.

"Heartbreaking? Of course. But I was watching his imagination, completely unfettered of the confines the rest of us think are necessary for living. It was either join in or lose my own mind."

Claire braced herself every time she visited her mother in the memory-care facility. She knew better than to ask whether her mother remembered who she was. The answer was too painful to hear.

But she visited regularly and carried on conversations as best as she could. She brought her mother small gifts, brushed her hair, painted her nails, and read to her.

"You're such a nice young lady," Claire's mother said one day. "I like you. I'm not sure why. But I'm glad you're here. Will you come see me again? What was your name again, dear?"

"Claire."

"I had a daughter named Claire."

"Is it okay with you if I think of you as my mom?"

A faint glimmer of light tiptoed close to the surface. "I suppose so. That would be nice." One of heaven's sweetest comforts is that we will "know as we are known."

"For now we see through a glass, darkly; but then face to face: now I know in part; but then shall I know even as also I am known," declares 1 Corinthians 13:12 (KJV).

Until then? We take comfort in the glimmers of light and the promise that God is with us, even in the agony of a parent who doesn't recognize who we are. We dance when there's no music playing. We check for land mines under the ottoman. And we dust the nightstand so our father's fingers can fly smoothly over its "keys."

"Don't be alarmed or terrified, because the LORD your God is with you wherever you go," Joshua 1:9 (CEB), reassures us.

Even if "wherever" is an octogenarian ballet recital or an imaginary golf tournament or a long-gone era.

Father God,
You know my name.
You'll always know my name
And who I am,
That I'm Your child.
Forever.

Protect my heart
From mortal blows
If the day should come
When the one I call Mom
Or the one I call Dad
Doesn't know what to call me.

CHAPTER TWENTY-ONE

When They Think Life No Longer Has Meaning

Life does not consist in the abundance of things;
nor, we could say, does it consist
in how we once measured significance.

My parents perfected the art of generosity," Alan said. "They gave without hesitation whenever they noticed a need. As is so often true," he added, "their generosity was a reflection of their heart, not of a fat bank account. They struggled like anyone else to pay their bills. Yet each of their children, half the community, and missions endeavors around the world benefited from their stepping in to financially help in times of distress.

"Not one of us mourned the loss of their physical gifts or monetary help once our parents were gone," Alan said. "We grieved that we couldn't imagine who else would pray for us the way they did."

Have you heard an aging parent say "I'm a worthless old person" or "I'm no use to anyone anymore"? Even if the statement is made in jest, it makes us cringe. Our efforts to convince our parents of that thought's blatant untruth are too seldom successful.

Linda, a woman I greatly admire, recently let me know that her thirty-year-old daughter is now in the presence of Jesus. The daughter hadn't spoken, fed herself, or sat under her own power since an accident stole those abilities from her when she was a toddler.

The mother stressed that it was a lie to claim her daughter's life as worthless. Linda's family measured value by the width of the young woman's crooked smile, the brightness in her eyes, the joy she found in vivid colors and the small details many of us miss in our striving in supposed accomplishments.

We might say, "Dad, Mom, your presence adds value to my life. Your wisdom is essential. Knowing you love me is more significant to me than anything else you achieved over the years."

"Even now?" an elderly or infirm parent might ask.

"Yes. Even now. In some ways, even more so now."

My eighty-six-year-old (as of this writing) neighbor, mentor, and friend Jackie was involved in a far-reaching radio ministry with me for more than three decades. The ministry began while she was raising her teenaged children and serving as a registered nurse. Eventually the ministry demanded more time, and she retired from nursing in order to devote more hours to it.

Her eyesight is now weaker than she'd like, after multiple complicated corneal transplants. Her legs are no longer strong enough to hold her without the aid of a walker. Her shoulders don't work as they should and cause constant pain. She leaves her house only when necessary—for doctor and dentist appointments or can't-miss family weddings or baby showers—and uses a wheelchair then. Even church attendance is too much for her worn-out body, despite her deep love for the Lord.

But she is more active than ever in exercising her

gifts. With other distractions gone, Jackie devotes herself to a prayer and encouragement ministry through e-mail, phone, and letters. The list of those for whom she consistently prays is long and weighty; the list of answered prayer equally long but buoyant.

Though housebound, she "accompanies" me to every speaking or teaching event through her prayers for me before, during, and after. "What time will you start speaking?" she asks, converting the answer into the proper time zone so she's sure to invest heavily in prayer at the moment I'm standing before the waiting audience.

The day before I leave for the event, she and I talk by phone so she can share a specific devotional encouragement she's gathered from her library of resources. Together we commit the final hours of preparation to God. She holds the rope that anchors me to hope.

I'm not the only person who says, "I want to be like Jackie when I grow up."

The older we get, the more we admire cultures that assume the elderly in a family or community are deserving of a high level of respect. Significance is not measured in accumulated wealth or level of corporate success. It is measured in longevity, endurance, and wisdom.

"You cannot get through a single day without having an impact on the world around you," says renowned anthropologist Jane Goodall. "What you do makes a difference, and you have to decide what kind of difference you want to make."

In what ways are we showing our aging parents that we value them, their counsel, their presence, their legacy?

"Mom, you make a difference with your kindness."

"Dad, you make a difference with the integrity you taught us, integrity you're still modeling."

"Your significance never was tied to your profession, Dad. Not in my eyes. It is and always was linked to the faith you lived in front of us—and still do."

"Mom, I've always appreciated how hard you worked to teach us life skills. I don't know where I'd be without them today."

"Dad, did I ever tell you that the neighbor kids were all jealous because I had a dad who wasn't afraid to do silly things, like jump on the trampoline in his pajamas and turn his shirt backward because mine was accidentally that way? I loved having a dad other kids admired. Thank you."

"I have been so blessed by parents who invested in my life at every stage, from kindergarten plays through college decisions through my career and my kids' lives. That's been priceless to me."

Our prayer is that such words—even if rebuffed initially—will resonate with our parents when they need to hear them, including days when they feel less than, unimportant, or useless.

God, thank You for loving us
When we had nothing more to offer
Than our devotion,
Fickle as it can be.
Thank You for infusing us
With worth
Because of Your Son's
Sacrifice.

Move through us
By Your Spirit
So that our faces,
Words,
And hearts
Convincingly express
Our parents'
Inexpressible worth
To us
And to You.

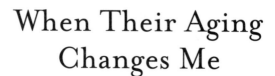

CHAPTER TWENTY-TWO

When Their Aging Changes Me

No child can watch a parent age
and remain the same person.

Does this journal entry from an anonymous friend read like a page from yours?

My father is a prisoner of war. He has all the earmarks. Gaunt, skeletal look. Thin, fragile skin that peels back to the touch. He doesn't open his eyes all the way. Or can't. Yet they bulge from his face like a frog squeezed too tight.

When I rub lotion on his back at night, his shoulder blades protrude like mountains of bone. The temptation is strong to press them back into position, if I weren't afraid they'd crumble under the pressure.

How long has it been since he's eaten more than a tablespoon of pureed whatever? It's not for lack of my trying.

As he wastes away, my muscles grow more defined. Or did. I'm a reluctant weight lifter whose routine involves hoisting fewer pounds each day. Dad's bulk is no longer a challenge to carry to the commode or back to bed. I can tell how much he's lost without a scale. And I now roll him onto his side one-handed. There's no comfort or pride in that.

He whispers his gratitude for every small kindness, as if he's waited all his life for someone to care about his needs, as if he's forgotten the years and tears and sleepless nights he invested in caring for me.

His tenderness slays me. It slices me open to lay bare a history of my harshness and irritation with him, holidays I thought were too full to fit in a cross-country trip to visit him, countless invitations to go fishing with him that I turned down to hang with friends whose names I no longer remember.

God, I haven't dared to ask for much from You. But I'm asking now that somehow You'll communicate through the mist of an aging mind and fill my father with glimpses of the joy that awaits him and with the assurance that he's loved. He's always been loved.

Even when I didn't know how to show it.

Our parents' aging—and their inevitable journey toward their story's end—changes us forever.

During the final years of my mom's slow crawl toward her last chapter, I felt her agony in my marrow. My breathing mirrored her shallow breaths. My chest ached as if it, too, were operating at 17 percent efficiency.

When she died, a different ache replaced those sympathy pains—the untouchable pain of deep loss.

But those weren't the only changes in me. My guess is that you would agree. Even in the earliest stages, when the signs are as innocuous as creases around their eyes or when they opt out of a project or activity once enjoyed or when they choose the ramp into the restaurant rather than the stairs—watching our parents show signs of aging shifts our thinking about the length of the dash of life, the space between date of birth and date of death.

I can no longer treat mortality as an offstage reality. I knew it was there somewhere, but it had no speaking parts until my parents' lives and illnesses invited it center stage.

The belief—rooted in love's fantasy—that my parents would be part of my life forever crumbled into bits too small to reconstruct. The realization hollowed me but also intensified my determination to make the most of moments, since they would forevermore seem too few.

My understanding about who my parents were at their core changed too. My father died before most normal aging processes could get a grip on him. If he'd lived long enough to lose his ability to play trumpet or teach or preach or feed his insatiable appetite for learning, I'm not sure any of us could have endured the despair that would have colored his days.

My mom's strong will had been forged. It wasn't a character flaw. It had been hammered on an anvil of life events that would have flattened most of us.

I saw my siblings in a new light too. Torchbearers. Charged with carrying on the legacy of loving parents with sterling work ethics, an abundance of empathy, an excess of generosity, and a relentless attitude of anticipation for heaven.

At one time, heaven's strongest pull for my mom was the idea of reuniting with her husband, mother, father, brothers, and sister. Toward the end, she spoke less of that reunion and more of her longing to see Jesus face-to-face. How could I not be changed by that reminder of heaven's crowning moment?

The transformations from watching a parent age include what we want to *avoid* when it's our turn, as well.

I've promised my children that I'll make every effort not to include a rehearsal of body functions in every conversation, to listen when they tell me they think I should see a doctor about that arrhythmia (or misshaped mole or hoarse cough), and to not lose my mouth's filter. I've asked them to hold me to it.

And I ask God to keep me lucid enough to comply.

How are you being changed by your parents' aging? In what ways are you maturing through this process? Are you resistant to the growth or embracing it?

The apostle Paul talks about "the renewing of our minds," a change in the way we think. In Romans 12:2 (CEB), he couples that counsel with its divine purpose—

"so that you can figure out what God's will is—what is good and pleasing and mature." The NIV version says, "Then you will be able to test and approve what God's will is—his good, pleasing and perfect will."

Is it possible that one of the by-products God intends to harvest in us during the season of our parents' aging is renewed thinking about life, death, significance, legacy, patience, kindness, gentleness, faithfulness . . . ?

Only by Your grace, Lord,
Will a rich harvest
Emerge
In this season.
Love—as I come to understand it
in deeper ways than before;
Joy—as I look for its presence among
the tangle of unpleasantries and loss;
Peace—as I embrace it as a prize worth pursuing
on behalf of those I love;
Patience—as those muscles become strong enough
to bear their necessity;
Kindness—as I witness the difference kindness makes;
Faithfulness—as I consistently refuse anything less;
Gentleness—as I pour it out and drink it in;
Self-control—as I use the filter I wish my parents had,
or adopt their noble habit.
Only by Your Grace.
Renew my mind
So the harvest
Pleases You.
Amen.

(Adapted from the fruit of the Spirit
listed in Galatians 5:22–23.)

CHAPTER TWENTY-THREE

When It's Just Plain Hard

God will not protect you from anything that will make you more like Jesus.

—ELISABETH ELLIOT

For all our talk about the privilege of serving our parents, the blessings of caring for them, the joys tucked among the challenges, we can't deny that, at times, caring for aging parents is excruciatingly hard.

"In her last years," Karen said, "Mom harmed herself by scratching and digging into her skin, causing huge wounds. She wouldn't stop for anything. We begged, pleaded, reasoned, and argued.

"Finally, we enlisted the aid of a wound-care specialist who wrapped the wounds (mostly on her legs and arms) in medicated wraps and materials that were cast-like. It would give her some relief, but then only hours after returning from the clinic, she would tear into those wraps and do more damage.

"I often found her in her bathroom or bedroom surrounded by blood. In her mental state, she thought there was something underneath her skin that she needed to get out. It was sad and heartbreaking and ghastly. Who can bear seeing their parent like that?"

Bryce said, "For some reason, Dad got it in his mind that we were stealing from him. It seemed ludicrous to us since he had little money that wasn't designated for paying his bills at the assisted-living facility. Ludicrous and gut-wrenching.

"My brothers and I were paying for many of his extra needs out of our own pockets, sacrificing time and a hundred other things to try to keep him comfortable. His suspicion of us was so hard to take. He stood firm in his conviction that one of us—or maybe all of us—had been stealing invisible money from his room. It was as real to him as the slippers on his feet."

Bryce and his family members knew it was a cruel figment of their father's malfunctioning imagination, a symptom typical of many elderly who suffer dementia issues. But that didn't suture the wounds their father's anger and suspicion sliced open.

Elizabeth enjoyed a comfortable relationship with her mother, even when her mom was well advanced in age. "I remember pushing her in a wheelchair through the flowers at the local garden center. She wanted to buy almost every plant she found.

"I helped her pick out three she liked. After our outing, we put the flowers on her porch at the nursing facility. She seemed so happy. It was one of the last days we had together when we had a good time.

"Her dementia worsened," Elizabeth recalled, "and I became—in her mind—an enemy, instead of her daughter.

"She's been gone for over seven years now. But each spring, as I roam through the plant section, I think of that one special day we had together."

Delores was put in an unenviable position. Her mother had been abusive all of Delores's life. But the court appointed her as guardian when her mother could no longer care for herself. "I did it because I was needed," she said.

"One day I took her for a drive to several spots where she'd grown up. When we got back to her house, she asked me to take off her shoes before I left to go home. As I knelt before her, she said, 'Thank you.' That's the first time I'd heard those words from her.

"Then she put her hand on my head and commented, 'Why is there silver in your hair?' I felt God's presence," Delores said, "in the benediction-like moment."

How sweet even small graces are when caring about or for our aging parents. How meaningful the love God enables us to show to those who don't always return it. How difficult but holy the sacrifices when there's pain in the offering.

"My caregiving for both my mother and my father started when I was a child," Elaine told me. "At eight years old, I was drafted into service because of my father's multiple heart attacks, a special-needs brother, and my mother's frail health. At thirteen, I balanced the checkbook and filed the family taxes in addition to physical caregiving."

That level of caregiving does not come without a price tag.

"As much as I loved my mother," Elaine said, "we were very dissimilar, and my heart's cry was for her to understand who I was . . . just me. She dismissed my desire to write as inappropriate and an unprofitable enterprise. She objected to my work in the theater and considered it unimportant. She grudgingly accepted my becoming a librarian but felt it wasn't the kind of job where I was really needed and I should be able to just take off if family required my time.

"I knew beyond a shadow of a doubt that she loved me, but she did not understand me. Then the roles reversed. Somewhere along the line, I made the choice to give her the kind of care and acceptance I had always wanted from her but felt was lacking. I discovered the truth behind what C. S. Lewis had to say about actions and love. Willfully acting toward another with good intent and kindness *produces* love."

"Christian love, either toward God or toward man, is an affair of the will. . . . Love in the Christian sense does not mean an emotion. It is a state not of feelings but of the will; that state of the will which we have naturally about ourselves and must learn to have about other people," says Lewis in his book *The Four Loves*.

Which of us from healthy homes would imagine a time when we might have to be intentional about loving our parents? That we might need to show kindness as an act of our will?

The rigors of caregiving, the soul-straining emotional price, can make us feel emotions we didn't think possible and face resentments we thought ourselves incapable of experiencing.

Why would God have made it a point to say, through the biblical writer, "Husbands, love your wives" (Ephesians 5:25 NIV)? Or "Love one another" (John 13:34 NIV)? Those verses are written as if love is a directive that can be followed rather than an emotion that is either present or isn't. And so it is.

Love—at its core—is more attitude than feeling. And the purest love is a response to God at work within us.

As our parents age, even the best relationships can fray at the edges or experience a seismic shift that splits hearts in two. *Feelings* of love threaten to slink away in the night, replaced by less-appealing obligation or tolerance.

It's easy to love when someone is loving toward us. But God said, in essence, that even the unbelieving know how to do that. If you love when it's not being returned, that's when it's remarkable.

"If you love only those who love you, what reward do you have? . . . Therefore, just as your heavenly Father is complete in showing love to everyone, so also you must be complete," Matthew 5:46, 48 (CEB).

God,
I never wanted to look at my parent
And say,
"Loving you
Is too hard
Right now."

But even
As I write these words,
I'm reminded
That's exactly
What You did.

You looked at me
And said,
"Loving you
Is too hard
Right now . . .
But I will
Anyway."

CHAPTER TWENTY-FOUR

When I Don't Know What to Say

Some teens have a hard time talking to their parents.
I didn't expect that kind of strain to return at this stage of life.

They just drive me crazy. Come every year. This year's the worst, though."

"What drives you crazy, Dad?"

"The bugs."

"Bugs?"

He shifted in his worn recliner. "Don't you see them outside the window? Ladybugs, I guess. They just drive me crazy. Come every year. This year's the worst, though."

"I see a few."

"Come every year. This year's the worst, though."

"Dad, have you seen much of Maureen?"

"Who?"

"Maureen. Your sister. My aunt."

"She died years ago. Such a wonderful woman. That was a sad, sad funeral. She was a wonderful woman."

"Dad, Maureen is alive. I spoke with her a week ago. She said she was planning to visit you last Sunday, if the weather was still good."

"Sunday? When was that?" The recliner creaked.

"Two days ago."

"Have you seen the bugs? Come every year. This year's the worst, though."

"Yes, they can be annoying. Did you go to the senior center for lunch today?"

"Oh, sure. Right after geometry. I'm not doing well in

that class. Numbers. Bah! Have you seen the bugs? Come every year. This year's the worst, though. By far."

"Yes, it is, Dad."

According to results of national studies conducted within the last decade and reported by *New York Times* columnist David Brooks, between a third and half of the current baby boomer population will suffer some form of dementia, from mild cognitive impairment to full-blown Alzheimer's.

What does a statistic like that do to us? It brings us to our knees with a soul-sobering reality only God can help us navigate.

When dementia issues move from statistics to our own parents or grandparents, we step into an altered universe that bears little resemblance to the familiar. As the disease or disorder progresses, we find ourselves not only giving, but giving *up* what we once cherished. We can no longer ask for advice. Family gatherings become a pinch-point of distress. Shared memories? Traditions? Inside family jokes that once caused instant laughter? Gone. Shelved. Relegated to a storage bin marked "Untouchable Past. Corrupted Disk. Irretrievable."

Conversation styles change.

One woman said, "I learned not to ask questions, because Dad would never know the answers and trying to find a suitable response brought him more frustration. So when I visited, rather than search for topics I hoped would be meaningful to him—and none were—I talked about relatively meaningless trivia that required no response.

"It exhausted me," she said, "but it filled the time we spent together and kept from aggravating his agitation that his brain wouldn't cooperate with conversation's natural give-and-take."

Mindy Peltier said of her grandmother, who lived in a memory-care facility, "After our visits, a few times she followed my children and me to the elevator and tried to get on. I used to think she wanted to come home with us, but now I know better. She wanted to escape, but she didn't know where she was from, so didn't know where to go.

"A staff member would gently hold her and talk in those reassuring tones they've perfected, while I pushed the button of GUILT and watched the doors close in front of her face."

For some, conversation is the one remaining connecting point. Other shared activities have diminished as the years progressed. "Sit and talk to me," a mom or dad might say. Behind those five simple words is a plea to share what still comes easily.

For others, conversation is difficult at best and nearly impossible at worst. A mental disconnect with reality, the disappearance of common ground for discussion, severe hearing issues, comprehension issues. . . .

Our minds race, searching for topics of discussion that will be of interest to our parents at this stage of their lives, for conversation starters that won't lead down tangled paths of frustration for us or them.

If your aging parents are comfortable conversationalists, consider yourself blessed.

If, instead, they struggle to respond verbally and are unable or hesitant to initiate conversation or if every discussion is caught in a spin cycle of sameness, my heart goes out to you.

"I've known caregivers to carry 'caregiver business cards' with them," Brent Mausbach, clinical psychologist at UC San Diego Health, says. These cards "state something like, 'My mother/father has Alzheimer's disease, and I am his caregiver. Please direct communication to me and know that he may (forget, be unable to communicate or answer questions, display agitation, etc.). Thank you for your patience.'"

The ability to verbally connect with our parents starts a handful of months after we're introduced to them— *Mama, Dada.* Our hope is that the connection would continue unbroken. But it doesn't always. And when their ability to communicate effectively ends, it adds another layer of heartbreak.

The gift of conversation with our parents parallels one aspect of the parent-child intimacy we can know with our heavenly Father. We talk. He listens. He talks. We listen. We read what He wrote and discover His true heart. Our communication with Him builds our faith.

When words won't come in our attempts to communicate with our aging parents, we can turn to the One who invites us to pour our hearts out to Him. May He fill us with hope-hemmed words to fill the empty spaces.

Reach out in the language Jesus speaks—the language of love.

"Let my mouth be filled with Your praise and with Your glory" (Psalm 71:8 NKJV).

Lord, I'm lost again.
Adrift.
Bereft
Of words.
No,
More than that . . .
Bereft of good words
That will warm
My parent's soul,
Light a spark
Of recognition.
And I tire,
I admit it,
Of carrying the full burden
Of conversation.
But I hear You say,
"Come
All who are weary."
I hear
Your Voice.
And it comforts me.

CHAPTER TWENTY-FIVE

When Time Is All They Want from Me

What a costly commodity—time!

One of the regrets from my adolescent days showed up with all the welcome of a recurrence of acne in menopause.

It's not easy to tell this story. But I probably need its reminder, even now. And you may find application for your situation with your aging parents.

For a number of reasons, some of which didn't emerge until after my parents were deceased, my mother worked full-time as a night nurse throughout the entirety of my childhood. She was an excellent nurse and devoted herself wholeheartedly to the profession, working extra shifts whenever needed.

As the oldest of five children, I may have felt the loss of her presence—her working all night and attempting to sleep during the day—most keenly. My siblings may disagree, and they have every right.

Dad worked long days. Mom worked long nights. Early in my childhood, I took over many of the responsibilities of homemaking and childcare for my younger brothers and sisters.

I don't regret all that. It formed much of my character, I'm sure, and equipped me with life skills that some of my friends didn't develop until after they were married.

But during my junior high and early high school years—maybe as a natural response to our circumstances, maybe because drama is never far from a junior higher's mind—the ache of not having Mom available like other mothers were, came to an inflamed head.

I longed for her time, not her paycheck.

That almost seems laughable now, because her paycheck was an absolute necessity. I had no doubt she loved me, but I wanted time with her and told her so—not with tender words, but in an eruption of teenage angst.

Years later, she would be the one begging for my time. Her world had been reduced to an eight-by-ten room at the end of a dark hall in a hospice aging facility.

And I had a choice to make.

God had softened my heart. I chose to give her what I felt I hadn't received. And we were both better for it.

As it is for many people, serving my mother was as much a spiritual endeavor as it was an act of love.

Her congestive heart failure created so many side complications for her. The system has changed now, but throughout the nine months Mom spent at the hospice residence facility, meals were a constant problem for her.

She'd lost her sense of smell and taste, so one would think it didn't matter what was on the plate in front of her. But it did.

Her body was so sensitive to salt that even a low-salt diet had too much sodium in it. The facility's contract for meals couldn't accommodate a no-salt diet. So Mom's choices were limited even further.

The only thing I could think to do was to prepare most of her food at home. I scoured the aisles of the grocery stores for cooking ingredients with no salt. Her appetite had dwindled to a few tablespoons of a casserole or a quarter cup of soup. But her mind's appetite appreciated variety and foods she'd always loved.

Loving her and obeying God included preparing and packing miniature-sized portions of "fancy" food—colorful, visually appealing, and healthy—which I hauled to the facility and left in their kitchen's freezer.

When the stockpile grew low, I'd go on the hunt in the grocery aisles again and do my best to create meals that would satisfy her but not tax her failing body.

I had a clear sense that the time it took to provide those meals was less chef-like and more "your spiritual act of service"-like, drawing the idea from Romans 12:1: "Therefore I urge you, brethren, by the mercies of God, to present your bodies a living and holy sacrifice, acceptable to God, which is your spiritual service of worship" (NASB).

Serving my mother held an air of holiness. In her last few days on earth, she often commented that Jesus was sitting in the corner of her room—just on the other side of the commode, which seemed highly inappropriate but tender at the same time.

Maybe the fact that she lived those months so close to the edge of eternity is what gave a perception that it was an act of worship, service to God, to take time to rub lotion on her back or keep searching for a strong-enough magnifying glass or set aside other responsibilities and prepare salt-free lasagna, which is no small feat.

Harriet Hodgson wrote of ten spiritual aspects of caregiving in a December 2015 blog post. You can probably think of more to add from your own experience with your aging parents.

Caregiving is love in action.
Caregiving makes us practice patience.
Caregiving causes us to look inward.
Caregiving links us with the past, present, and future.
Caregiving makes us aware of the joy of giving.
Caregiving leads us in new directions.
Caregiving is a learning experience.
Caregiving brings out the best in us.
Caregiving helps us see what is important.
Caregiving honors the miracle of each and every life.

I might amend a point or two, noting that caregiving brings out both the best *and* the worst in us and sometimes is the vehicle God uses to take us to a place where our hearts need to be.

Of the things
That occupy my time, Lord,
Serving my parents
For their sake
And in Your name
May be
The most honorable,
Challenging,
And soul-satisfying
Of all.

CHAPTER TWENTY-SIX

When Guilt Taints
Our Relationship

Guilt—the tattered rag we try to throw away,
but the dog thinks we're playing fetch.

A lot of my guilt stems from my mother's last six months or so," a friend confessed. "After a long hospital stay, the doctors wanted her to go to a rehab center. So we let them put her in a rehab/nursing facility.

"I know it's the right answer for many people, but I couldn't stand for her to be there. She was alone and so small. I wanted to bring her home. The staff talked me out of it every time. I knew I couldn't give her the nursing care she needed and couldn't lift her, but I hated that she was there.

"Then one night, I fell down the stairs and broke my leg. I had to have surgery and was bedridden for several months. That was bad enough, but I couldn't go to see my mom.

"When I finally was able to visit her in my wheelchair," she added, "the shock was hard to bear. She had declined so much. I desperately wanted to bring her home . . . but now I was wheelchair-bound.

"She died a few weeks later. I'm still dealing with the guilt of not being there for her. Yes, I know, it couldn't be helped. Guilt doesn't listen to that kind of reasoning."

Stephen bore endless regrets about his relationship with his estranged father. He'd tried many times to reconcile over the years. Eventually Stephen stopped trying. How much battering could his pride take?

He'd hoped age might soften his father's heart, that

forgiveness would come easier to the old man as his life drew closer to its end. But instead, the hardwood of his heart petrified. And his ability to communicate was the first of his functions to leave.

Stephen and his father's unfinished business remained unfinished. "I could have tried one more time before it was too late." The guilt-laden words loop through Stephen's mental playlist.

Jolene remembers, "My daughter's destination wedding in the Bahamas had been in the planning stages for a year when my mother took ill. The doctors assured us she'd be okay but wouldn't be ready to travel.

"My daughter and her husband-to-be volunteered to postpone the wedding until Mom could join us. But we all knew rearranging so many schedules and paying cancellation fees at that late date would have been cumbersome, to say the least.

"Mom insisted we go through with our plans, that she would be content to watch the video after the fact.

"We got the call in the middle of the wedding reception. Mom had fallen, an apparent stroke, and never recovered. I held that news to myself until the reception was over, thinking—how foolish of me—that waiting would spare my daughter the grief of knowing her grandmother died while she danced with her new husband.

Jolene couldn't stop her tears. "Even now I don't know.

Should we have canceled the plans? Would that have been the right thing to do? Would it have made a difference? Could we have stopped Mom from falling? Prevented her life-ending stroke? I don't know. But it's taking everything in us to fight off guilt over our decisions."

"After my mom died," Marla said, "I was advised not to go in to see her body; people knew I'd been so close to her. But a future of guilt-ridden regrets wouldn't let me follow that advice. Touching her ice-cold hand and stroking her forehead for the last time was something I will never forget. I would never see her face again on this earth. I'm glad I have that closure, that touchstone, if you will.

"Now I know why elephants are so insistent to keep their dead comrades and family close for a time after their deaths," Marla said. "When they are deprived of this opportunity to see, to touch, to know . . . to mourn, they are unsettled and worrisome. I spared myself in that brave moment, going against all well-meaning advice."

What do we do when aging-parent guilt clings to us like sharp-edged barnacles, scraping us and others as we brush past? Logic can't make it fall away. On an intellectual level, we know we can't meet our aging parents' every need. But we take on the guilt as if we should at least try.

Dementia, at least, removes the ability to reason, so when a parent lashes out in confusion or anger, it should be automatic for us to resist unwarranted guilt over what we said, did, didn't say, or didn't do to cause the outburst. But it *isn't* easy. It's anything but automatic to fight off guilt.

Caring for aging parents often means juggling responsibilities between aging parents and at-home children, or aging parents and job demands, or aging parents and a spouse's medical needs. It's a season of choosing one over the other, shuffling heartaches, triaging disasters. *Kyle's appendectomy takes precedence over Mom's broken hip, right? Okay, my husband can stay with Kyle while I make sure Mom's new care team understands her medical history. I can't win. I want to be with Kyle too.*

What kind of people would we be if these tensions didn't disturb us?

From our perspective, meeting the needs of those we care about will sometimes afford us no good options. Not surprisingly, someone—if not all parties—will be disappointed by our decision and our triage prioritizing.

- Is the heart of my problem that I'm worried about how other people will perceive me or that I'll lose my reputation as the person who can juggle it all?
- Is pride keeping me from seeking God's intervention? Do I assume I ought to be able to figure out a solution on my own, so if I turn to God, that's a sign of defeat?

- Is pride keeping me from enlisting the help of others?

Guilt—if untended—gets in the way. It's as hazardous to relationships and spiritual health as a ball and chain tethered to a long-distance swimmer. God made provision in His Word for dealing with guilt and its troublemaking sidekick, pride.

Psalm 51:1–2 (CEB) is the expression of the psalmist David's heart. In his case, his guilt was well-placed. But even for those of us who know our guilt is unfounded, its sweet comfort can serve as a balm to our soul.

"Have mercy on me, God, according to your faithful love! . . . Wash me completely clean of my guilt."

Father God,
Caring for aging parents
Is consuming.
It's an inconvenient time
For guilt
To want my attention.

So with Your help
I'll let You handle it
When it insists
On camping
In my heart.

CHAPTER TWENTY-SEVEN

When My Parents' Needs Cost Me

There's no longer give-and-take in the relationship.
Only give and give some more.

—MINDY PELTIER

Bonnie watched her daughter Ella lift five-week-old Zoe to her shoulder for the important post-meal burp. Three generations cozied in the family room, with a fourth napping down the hall.

"Is Zoe sleeping any better?"

Ella's sigh paused in the middle before it released in a slow, telling exhale. "Zach spoiled me. He slept through the night before we left the hospital."

"I remember. And I also remember telling you not to rely on it with all your babies."

"I doubted you then. Paying for it now." Ella yawned.

"Want me to watch her for a few hours so you can get a nap?"

"Mom, who's going to do that for *you?* From the dark circles under your eyes, I'd guess Grandma is still getting you up a lot at night."

Bonnie leaned over her knees, stretching tense muscles. She stayed bent and said, "I'd sell a kidney for a solid night's sleep."

"I hear you." Ella adjusted Zoe, who had mastered the secret of daytime sleeping and proved it. "Intellectually, I know I'll live through this temporary sleep deprivation."

"Me too." Bonnie righted herself. "But there are days when I wonder if my breaking point isn't nearer than I thought."

Ella closed her eyes and leaned her head against the sofa's backrest. "We're orbiting in parallel universes. We're both changing diapers, losing sleep, responding when someone we love cries out for no good reason, exhausting ourselves caring for the helpless. . . ."

"Your charge," Bonnie said, "will grow more independent. Mine will grow more dependent until the day when she'll abruptly not need me anymore."

"Mom. . . ."

"I told you once to view those middle-of-the-night feedings as a tender opportunity for alone time with your baby. Just the two of you, whispering your love in your own ways as you snuggle and rock in the dark."

"I'm trying to take that to heart."

"I think God's telling me I'm supposed to do the same. When your grandmother calls for me in the middle of the night and I groan my way out of bed to see what she needs, I should apply my own advice and treasure that time between the two of us. But that gets harder and harder the more exhausted I get. Ella? Ella?"

Bonnie rose from her chair and tucked a chenille throw around her daughter and granddaughter, who were lost in their dreams, locked in love.

I was a young mom with a sleep-resistant infant when someone pointed me to the verse in Psalms that tells us, "God wants his loved ones to get their proper rest" (Psalm 127:2 TLB).

I was a middle-aged woman lying on a loveseat inches away from my dying mother when the verse circled around again. "Go home and rest," the hospice caregivers told me.

How could I consider sleep when my mom was fighting so hard to draw her next breath?

And how do we survive one more day when we feel as if we've reached the end of our energies and tolerance?

How does the mother of a newborn survive weeks or months on a fraction of the sleep she needs?

How do we keep giving to aging parents who need us when we are sure we have nothing left to give?

A hymn writer answered this way:

When we have exhausted our store of endurance,
When our strength has failed ere the day is half done,
When we reach the end of our hoarded resources
Our Father's full giving is only begun.
His love has no limits, His grace has no measure,
His power no boundary known unto men;
For out of His infinite riches in Jesus
He giveth, and giveth, and giveth again.
—Annie Johnson Flint

The author who penned those words—holding a pen, not a computer keyboard—spent much of her adult life in a wheelchair, unable to walk, her hands distorted by pain and crippling arthritis.

Annie Johnson Flint slept at night surrounded by nine pillows, placed just so, to help alleviate distress to her joints. The foreword of her biography notes that the arrangement was an attempt at "protecting the exquisitely sensitive, pain-smitten body from the normal contact of the bed clothing, so distressing it was for her to recline in the hope of rest at night" (Philip E. Howard, president of The Sunday School Times Company, Philadelphia, Pennsylvania).

The poetry from which this hymn was written is one of the treasures my grandmother kept in a thin leather journal she'd started when she taught in a one-room schoolhouse, the kind of classroom Annie J. Flint would have served if arthritis hadn't interrupted her plans to teach and exhausted her life. Her spirit was not exhausted, however.

As I reread those pain-penned words today, I knew the answer to the question of how we keep going when we think we can't be the caregiver any longer.

We lean on friends who offer respite care.

We lean on the support of our church family, even for an hour or two.

We lean on family members who need caregiving practice.

And we lean on the One who gives more grace.

"He will shelter me in his own dwelling during troubling times; he will hide me in a secret place in his own tent; he will set me up high, safe on a rock" Psalm 27:5 (CEB).

"Lean on Me"
Has never meant
So much
As it does now, Lord,
When You whisper it
Over my tired soul.

CHAPTER TWENTY-EIGHT

When I Feel as if the Battle Is Mine Alone

*Caregiving and loneliness
share an excess of common ground.*

An infrequently referenced story in the Bible illustrates that caring about and for the elderly in their last years is not for the faint of heart. The custom embedded in the story may seem curious to modern minds, especially for those unfamiliar with the culture of biblical times.

First Kings 1:1–4 (CEB) tells us that King David had grown old. Old-old. Very old. Feeble. Weak. Close to death. "His servants covered him with blankets, but he couldn't stay warm. They said to him, 'Allow us to find a young woman for our master the king. She will serve the king and take care of him by lying beside our master the king and keeping him warm.'"

That's the curiosity, although later in that chapter the biblical text makes it clear that the concept was purely for comfort and not for physical intimacy. Some commentators suggest that David's physicians thought the young woman's vitality might revive him as she served her role as practical nurse and, well, human blanket.

Next comes the part with which we can better identify: "So [the servants] looked in every corner of Israel until they found Abishag from Shunem" (verse 3).

They looked everywhere. In every corner. They searched diligently to find someone fitting for this assignment, someone both caring and willing to make the sacrifices that were asked of the young woman.

Caregiving is a hard, consuming, isolating assignment, even with the most pleasant parent and for those in the most loving of relationships. Caregiving takes a toll, whether the caregiving is from a distance or in-home, full-time or part-time. As if the heart is ever off duty.

Caregiving has traditionally been handled by women, but more men are assuming that responsibility. "As illnesses progress in loved ones, family caregivers become increasingly responsible for hands-on care, such as assisting with bathing and hygiene, as well as cooking, cleaning, and managing bills," says Karla Washington, assistant professor with the University of Missouri's department of family and community medicine.

"This extra load of responsibility can cause serious stress in a caretaker's life," Washington added. Researchers found that of the 280 family caregivers studied, women "had much lower self-esteem, less family support, and more harmful consequences in terms of their health and schedules than men."

A study published by *JAMA [Journal of American Medical Association] Internal Medicine* concluded that "caregivers who provided substantial medical help were more likely to report emotional, financial, and physical difficulties than those who provided no medical help. Additionally, they were more than five times more likely to report having trouble making time for enjoyable activities and three times more likely to report worse job productivity."

Job productivity. Yes. A majority of those heavily involved in caregiving also hold jobs.

Joyce says, "When my parents considered moving to Mississippi, it was with the thought of taking care of their own parents as they grew older. We had no idea my mother would need our tender, loving care.

"She had severe headaches for several months before finally going to the doctor. They discovered a brain tumor. Following surgery, she returned home and was progressing well.

"But she began to experience the same symptoms again. Another brain tumor and another surgery. Both tumors, she was told, were benign.

"As she was recovering in the hospital," Joyce said, "her hip began to hurt. She was diagnosed with bone cancer. I cannot tell you how the mental, physical, and emotional toll affected all of us.

"Through the process you learn, you pray, and you hope. My dad was very gracious and tender toward my mother. We faced it together. We gathered around her bed and prayed with her with tears. Our lives were changed, but our faith was not."

"So many treated me like some kind of saint because

I wanted to help care for my mother. I did it because it was the right thing to do! The fact that she was so precious made things easier," said one loving daughter.

"Hospice folks told me I would be the winner out of this whole ordeal, and they were right. The Lord taught us all so much about each other, about trusting Him, and the importance of making the most of each day.

"This has been the hardest year of my life, but I would not have traded the opportunity to be there for my mother."

If we stew because we have no help but we haven't *asked* for help—from family members, friends, our church, or the community—or described how isolated we feel in caring for our parent, then we've skipped a vital communication step.

If we've asked repeatedly and received no response, rather than letting the lack of response ratchet up our stress level, it's time to turn to other resources.

As unsettling as it might feel initially, adult children of aging parents who search out a support group, in-person or online, find others with similar concerns who can offer understanding, ideas, and a reminder that they're not alone.

Every caregiver needs a listening ear. It might be a spouse, a friend, or, if necessary, a counselor. Some advisors add that the listening ear doesn't necessarily have to be of the human variety. (And by that, I mean a pet. Aliens make poor listeners. Or so I've heard.)

One of God's most oft-repeated comforts for His children has direct application for adult children caring tirelessly for aging parents: "Don't be afraid, for I am with you" (Isaiah 41:10 NLT).

The feeling that we are alone is an inaccuracy. He is there with us in the middle of it all.

With me even here, Lord?
When I have to turn my eyes away
Because my parents' hands tremble
And I know they will not stop?

With me even here, Lord?
When he can't remember how to swallow
And I'm coaching my father
In a task he cannot master?

With me even here, Lord?
When my mother tells me
She wishes she'd been able
To have children?

With me even here, Lord?
When I'm performing tasks
Better suited to a newborn
Than a parent?
Even here?

"Lo, I am with you always"
(Matthew 28:20 NASB).

CHAPTER TWENTY-NINE

When I Can't Keep My Promise to My Parents

Caring for aging parents
challenges the meaning of devotion.

"Daddy wanted his ashes scattered on the gymnasium floor where he and his buddies played three-on-three until they were well into their seventies," Bob said. "On his deathbed, he made me promise I'd take care of the matter.

"Who could keep a promise like that? For one thing, the school frowned on it—in a legal way. I was foolish to make the promise. But he was so insistent, so frail and agitated, and I didn't want to dishonor him."

Bob paused in his storytelling. "I hope he was okay with Plan B. And I hope one day I'll be able to live with myself for breaking that promise to my father."

I never heard the end of that story.

"Just wrap me up in an old rug and set me out at the curb on garbage pickup day. I don't need no fancy casket."

"Mom, I can't make a promise like that."

"It's what I want. Shouldn't I be able to have what I want at my age?"

No. The answer is no.

"Promise me no flowers."

"I can't promise that other people won't send flowers for your funeral."

"Promise me I can die here at home. Not in the hospital."

The adult child draws a deep breath. "I'll try."

"Promise me."

God, keep us from asking impossible promises of our children when we reach that stage of life.

Like a heartbroken parent forcing a child to wear corrective leg braces, the caregiving adult child has to rise above the tears and the lump in his or her throat to make difficult decisions, decisions that may frustrate or anger the aging parent. In most cases, there is truly no other option than the one that a caring son or daughter makes.

How do we emotionally survive that? And how do we know when it's time to stand firm and say, "Mom, Dad, I cannot do what you're asking of me."

- Stay connected to God. He's our strength, stability, and fortress in time of trouble, including decision-making trouble (Jeremiah 16:19; Psalm 18:2; 31:3; 144:2).
- Pray. Commit the crisis to God's care. He knows better than we do and better than the experts we consult. His wisdom is dependable, reliable, and infallible (James 1:5).
- Don't take personally any resistance, depression, or anger the ill parent presents. It's the disease or disability that speaks harsh words against us. Paranoia and depression often accompany dementia and other aging conditions that force us to make decisions about our parents' care.

- Be sensitive to the parent's needs and desires as much as reasonably possible. Our own convenience will not be the primary determination. It never was. Our understanding of God's express will, sought through much prayer and surrender, makes the ultimate choice.

- Honor the parent's wishes when appropriate, even if it's not what we would choose. That counsel can apply many years before end of life.

If Mom or Dad wants to eat breakfast at eleven, lunch at two, and supper at four . . . on a lid from a plastic ice cream pail, is that worth fighting over? If they want to wear fluorescent socks, should that be a point of contention between us? Retaining the right to make choices can go far in bolstering an elderly parent's sense of self-worth.

And when the unkept promise is heart-wrenching?

Joy had taken so much time off work to be by her mother's side during her illness, that now her job was in jeopardy. She discussed her mother's condition with the medical staff, who advised that they had no way of determining how long her mother would hold on.

"Do you think I could safely go home this afternoon and take care of a critical overseas conference call? I can be back here within three or four hours."

"We really can't say. She could last another two weeks. Or two months. Or two minutes."

Joy knew she had to try. Her job was helping pay for her mother's care. She kissed her mother good-bye and promised to be right back, her heart clenching at her mother's plaintive cry—"Don't go"—that followed her out the door.

The doctors later told Joy that her mother was probably gone before Joy reached the city limits. She'd been at her mother's side constantly, but not at the moment of her death. And the burden of that truth tore at her.

How could she live with the ultimate betrayal, putting the needs of her job above the needs of her mother?

Only one way. Forgive herself.

Others tried to comfort her, telling her it may have been that her mother was waiting for a moment when she and Jesus were alone. Or that it was a no-win decision. Either way, Joy would have regretted the outcome.

Ultimately, when we fail to or can't keep a promise to our parents, we have only one option—to forgive ourselves and trust that what we consider a gross offense is not a subject of conversation for the loved one who has crossed to a world that knows no disappointment.

It shouldn't surprise me, Jesus,
That I've failed to keep some promises.
You're the only One of us
Who managed to reach
The end of Your earth-life
With all promises kept.

It's no wonder
I have no other place
To turn
Than You
When I'm faced with decisions
That rattle me
And hold the potential
To disappoint my parents.

Cover me, Lord.
Cover me.

CHAPTER THIRTY

When I Don't Recognize or Like Who My Parent Has Become

Don't let their expertise at making you feel miserable make you feel miserable.

Daniel drew a deep breath before sharing his story.

"My father was a good Christian man. Had a great sense of humor that he passed on to me. Tall like me. As a child, I thought he was perfect. As I grew into an adult, I saw that he wasn't perfect, but I still looked up to him and respected him.

"In his later years, I saw a number of changes in him that eventually led me to feel ashamed of him. His gentleness became a harshness that often seemed cruel. His humility became a need to be recognized for every accomplishment, real or imagined. He'd once given God glory and now stole it.

"Dad became judgmental and self-focused. I would say I hardly recognized him, but I knew who he was—my father. And I found myself despising him at times.

"He wasn't the man I had looked up to years before. I hoped and prayed we'd see his attitude return to that of the man I admired. But he died three weeks after my wife and I left the country for our first term as missionaries.

"On the other hand," Daniel said, "my mother is just as sweet or sweeter than she was in her younger years. She's ninety-three and in assisted living. She's joyful all the time. Appreciative of the smallest kindness.

"God has blessed her with great contentment and peace in her final years. That is an indescribable comfort to me."

Michelle said, "As my parents aged, 'Honor your mother and father' created both peace and fear—but ultimately it was the right answer every time."

Remember the children's book, *Are You My Mother?* by P. D. Eastman? A baby bird broke through his egg while his mother was out searching for food. The baby bird set out on a journey to find his mom, asking a kitten, a hen, a cow, and a dog, "Are you my mother?" The bird asked a number of inanimate objects too. The question "Are you my mother?" propelled him forward.

Toward the end of my mom's life, she expressed a handful of irrational fears. I felt the question rise within my soul, "Are you my mother? My mother wasn't afraid of anything!"

Gregarious parents who become reclusive, cultured and proper parents who grow sloppy and coarse with age, kind parents who become cruel or the courageous who become timid or the strong who grow frail. . . .

"Are you really my mother? My father? I hardly recognize you."

Years ago, they probably listened to a teenaged child's rantings, wild ideas, and irrational fears and said to themselves, "Are you my child? I hardly recognize you."

The teen years were a season—rockier for some of us more than others. Aging-parent years are a season as well, a season of indeterminate length.

Who were our parents in their prime? At their best? Who are they at their core? How can we focus on and preserve their true legacy rather than the shadow of who they once were, or an illness- and age-shaped imitation of the real thing?

"It's a choice. Like love is a choice," Ken says. "I choose to fill my mind with memories of the days when my father was a strong force of nature in my life. When I walk away from his room in our home, my ears stinging from the angry words he's hurled at me, I mentally wash my hands at the door, rinsing down the drain what just happened so I can get a good grip again on who my father really is, if it weren't for his aging issues.

"I don't pretend it's easy," he says. "But it's protective for both of us."

Tanya grieves over what dementia did to her sweet-tempered father. When the disease became full-blown, the man who hadn't cursed a day in his life became foul-mouthed and hostile. He'd been one of the gentlest men Tanya had ever met. But the disease stripped all the gentle-ness away and left him a raging animal, twisting his face into distortions that made it painful for her to visit him and ashamed when anyone else did. His friends said they understood it was the disease. But they soon stopped coming.

Karen watched her mother slowly morph into a person

she fought to tolerate and barely recognized. "I'm not proud of how I felt about her toward the end," she says. "It was a hard, hard journey. For both of us."

She tells about the day when her husband took her to the rehab center where her mother resided at the time.

"We arrived at lunchtime, so I was able to feed her. My mother had become so weak and was nearly blind too. Then my husband wheeled me (I was in a wheelchair, recuperating from a broken leg) and her (she was in a wheelchair too) out to the high-ceilinged lobby where the rehab-center staff had installed a twenty-five-foot Christmas tree.

"Mother and I sat in those wheelchairs in front of the tree for several hours. What a rare time! She was lucid, aware of who I was, asking about the family, laughing, talking, and almost seeming like she had been before she started declining. It was the sweetest time. I know it was a gift from God. She died in her sleep that night."

Karen ended her story with these words: "God, help me to remember her the way she was that night and the way she was when she was healthy. I'm rolling the unpleasant memories onto Your shoulders. I can't bear them."

"The LORD is good," reads Nahum 1:7 (CEB), "a haven in a day of distress. He acknowledges those who take refuge in him."

No matter how adult we perceive ourselves to be, we're never too old to crawl up into the lap of God and find a haven there. The soul-deep challenges we face as our parents age provide more than enough reason to seek comfort in His embrace.

Would you hold me closer tonight, Lord?
When I try to sleep,
I'm troubled by reminders
Of the hot anger
In my sweet mother's eyes
Or the sting of my father's
Harsh words against his caregiver.
Hold me closer, Lord.
I miss the people they were.
Tonight, all I have is You.
And yes,
You are enough.
But if You could give me
Other images
To cushion my sleep,
I'd be grateful.

CHAPTER THIRTY-ONE

When I Become the Story-Keeper

Generous listening is powered by curiosity,
a virtue we can invite and nurture
in ourselves to render it instinctive.

—Krista Tippett

When I visited my ninety-something maternal grandfather in the nursing home, I could count on two things. His soft gray eyes would tear up at some point during the visit. He had such a tender heart. And he would somehow work into the conversation that he had held the record for the hundred-yard dash at his hometown school since he was a teenager in 1914.

"Never been broken to this day," he'd say.

It apparently had been broken, at some point. No one had the heart to let him know. Smart people.

An elderly neighbor had an arsenal full of stories but especially liked telling ones about his part-time job in a monkey lab during his college years. The night the monkeys escaped from their enclosures . . . well, no one could tell the story like he could.

We heard the stories of the night my nurse mom delivered twins and the night she delivered a preemie, small and blind and not expected to live, but whom Mom was determined would not only survive but see. And she did.

It wasn't until Mom was in her late seventies that I heard the story—or was finally listening—about the night I was born. At the time, women would often labor in a ward with ten or eleven other laboring women. The hospital was short-staffed that night. Mom's nursing skills came in handy.

A woman was ready to give birth, but no doctor or nurse was available. So Mom got out of her bed, waited for one of her own contractions to pass, then instructed the woman to push. Mom caught the baby, took care of suctioning its airways, cut the cord, finished the delivery, and returned to her own bed.

And it happened again that night. My mother delivered *two* babies while waiting for me to be born. The babies were strong and healthy, the mothers grateful. But my mom joked that she was a little disappointed neither new mom named their child Dorothy, after her.

They were both boys.

That quick-thinking, what-do-you-need-let-me-help, between-contractions story so describes the person my mother was.

She also told the story—hesitantly—of having been accosted during nurses' training by a deranged patient. He almost succeeded in choking her to death. It explained why she hated anything around her throat, decades later.

Our family heard the story of my maternal grandfather as a young man, standing in the field and making hay, when his father came charging down the dirt road at the bottom of the hill with my grandfather's sister and a local doctor in the buggy. He'd been warned not to take the bridge at the bottom of the hill. It was in need of repair.

My great-grandfather, his responses skewed by what he'd been drinking in town, ignored the warning. The bridge collapsed. The doctor and the young girl—my great-aunt Rhoda—were killed while her brother watched and screamed from the top of the hill.

Knowing the story explained some of the pain that circled my grandfather's kind eyes and would suddenly sober his laughter long years after the event. My mother says he never spoke of his father.

My mom's brother Roger was part of the reason Mom decided to become a nurse. He'd suffered excruciating headaches that were later determined to be brain tumors. A strong, broad-shouldered farm boy became bedridden with a prognosis that shook the family.

Roger was near death when Mom laid her newborn daughter—me—in his arms. The way Mom told it, he calmed and settled, a wide smile on his tortured face when he held me. I had nothing to offer him. Maybe it was the reminder of new life that calmed him. Heaven's version of new life called him not long after.

What's the story you've heard so often from your parents or grandparents that you can tell it word for word, inflections, dramatic pauses, and all? Are there multiple stories?

When my widowed mother-in-law visited recently, we asked her to share stories of her parents and grandparents.

She said, "My mother and father rarely talked about their parents. I know so little about them, except that my grandfather emigrated to America due to a little trouble he'd gotten into gambling." She raised her eyebrows. That was the end of the story.

She and her sister had made some preliminary attempts to trace the history of the family when they were younger but ran into dead ends. And now, those who might have once known a bit of information to aid the search are gone.

Is there a story-keeper in your family? Someone who listens and probes and writes down the curiosities and courageous moments in your family history for when the stories stop coming? Shouldn't every family have at least one story-keeper?

Like too many of us, I didn't pay attention the way I should have when the stories were flowing, when grandparents were vital and their memories sharp. Why is it that so often our fascination with the stories of our family's past doesn't kick in until those who know the stories well are fading in their ability to tell them? By the time we're ready to listen, the storytellers have lost the details—or even the main points.

Or they're already gone, taking the rich stories with them.

God anticipated that danger in His children, so He

appointed storytellers, instructing His people, "Write this down. Record this for future generations. Tell those yet to be born."

"Let this be written down for the next generation so that people not yet created will praise the LORD," reads Psalm 102:18 (CEB).

Purposeful remembering is important to God. It appears more than 160 times in the Bible.

In Deuteronomy 32:7, God specifically encourages us to remember, to recount, to recollect, to meditate on the stories the elderly have to share with us in regard to the way the Lord has dealt with them. "Remember the days of old; consider the generations long past. Ask your father and he will tell you, your elders, and they will explain to you" (NIV).

We are a storytelling people. A high percentage of us learn best through story.

Who's your family storyteller? Who's the one who tells God's stories? Who's the story-keeper?

God, let me be
The berry-picker
Who wisely glances back
From where she's been
To see the hidden bursts
Of storied color
Tucked among the leaves
Of the past.

CHAPTER THIRTY-TWO

When Visiting Deepens My Pain . . . and My Understanding

When a father gives to his son, both laugh;
when a son gives to his father, both cry.

—William Shakespeare

A nd you visited Me."

Jesus said those heart-tugging words to people who had missed the connection that when we serve others, it's as if we're serving Him. They were—like we often are—diligently engaged in impressive projects of study and speaking, talking about God's Word, memorizing what God said, and giving generously.

But Jesus stopped their rehearsal of all they'd done for Him when He said this in Matthew 25:42–45 (CEB):

> "I was hungry and you didn't give me food to eat. I was thirsty and you didn't give me anything to drink. I was a stranger and you didn't welcome me. I was naked and you didn't give me clothes to wear. I was sick and in prison, and you didn't visit me.
>
> Then they will reply, "Lord, when did we see you hungry or thirsty or a stranger or naked or sick or in prison and didn't do anything to help you?"
>
> Then he will answer, "I assure you that when you haven't done it for one of the least of these, you haven't done it for me."

I'm one of the people He was talking about two thousand years ago. I'm one who finds it much easier to let someone else do the hospital visitation, visit the nursing home, or stop by at the assisted-living facility to spend time with an aging friend or relative. And my excuses have included "I don't know what to say"; "I don't want to interrupt the patient's sleep"; "I'm not comfortable."

Those excuses fall away one by one in light of Christ's viewpoint. *Comfortable* has nothing to do with it. I'm to wait on God if I don't know what to say. Just sit there quietly. But show up.

It can be an especially difficult task when visiting the people most precious to us—our aging parents. We hate admitting it, but awkward or painful moments sometimes take center stage.

Their pain disturbs us. Their physical infirmities crush us. When they lose their ability to communicate freely, the effort exhausts us. Their illness-driven anger or hostility bruises us.

And that's the problem. *Us.*

We approach visiting our parents with a completely natural focus on how it affects our personal barometric pressure. What does the visit do to us?

With our mouths, we say, "Anything for you, Jesus." But when He asks, "Will you visit Me in the nursing home?" we retreat into, "I'm sorry. I didn't understand the question."

You may be one who finds it pure joy to visit with the elderly and infirm. You may be one who has never resisted Christ's call or your parents' need. God bless you.

Sincerely. You're to be commended for your gifts and how you use them, for your selflessness and your servant heart.

But others of us may need to remember that shoving the barriers of difficulty or uneasiness out of the way will allow us to respond to the need as Jesus would. This is not only an act of God-given courage; it ministers directly to Jesus as well. What a privilege to serve our parents and the King in one move!

On the practical side, experts on aging advise that where once conversation alone could carry the day during a family gathering, that may no longer be the case, as our parents age.

They suggest engaging both the mind and the spirit as the body declines, through shared crossword puzzles, Scrabble, riddles, trivia, brainteasers, Bible stories, and the like, when appropriate. Try crafting projects. Create memory albums together. Listen to your parents' favorite music. Read to your parent. Invite grandchildren to read to their grandparent.

When memory loss and mental acuity grow too weak for some of those activities, bringing coffee-table-style library books of garden scenes, landscapes, artwork, or fabric arts can help make the visit meaningful.

We falsely assume that visiting our parents should feel natural. We're family. We've known each other all our lives. We've built a unique history together.

But we haven't known our parents like this—with this cocktail of physical ailments and aging issues. And we bring to the visit a retooled, revised package of concerns and responsibilities. It's new, unfamiliar territory. And it may require a level of creativity unnecessary in past stages of shared life.

Janet used to feel the tension rising as the minutes ticked by while she visited her father. Her visceral reaction happened even when she focused on staying calm, both when he still lived in his home and after he was transferred to a facility where he could get the specific medical attention he needed.

"I felt as if lapses in our conversation were my fault and that if I loved my father as I should, being with him wouldn't cause stress. Which caused me more stress."

She stumbled onto a partial solution accidentally, when she found Scotty, one of her dad's coworkers from his railroading days, in the chair she usually occupied. Janet pulled another chair to the table where Scotty and her father were sitting and staring at a checkerboard, mid-game. The three-way conversation added a layer of ease Janet hadn't known when she visited solo.

"Are one of you going to make a move?" she asked the men.

"Well," Scotty said, "I'm already married, and he's your father, so I guess your answer is no, young lady."

Janet's father smiled for the first time in a long time. At a snail's pace, he slid a black checker one space forward, then turned and winked at his daughter.

"The moment of near normalcy did so much for my soul," Janet said. "And I could tell it blessed Dad too. He seemed to enjoy listening to Scotty and me talk about our children, what was happening 'out there' in the world. It was as if he felt relieved to have the burden of carrying half the conversation lifted from his shoulders, since stringing words together in a way that made sense taxed him so heavily."

From that day on, Janet often took one of their mutual friends, a grandchild, or a neighbor with her when she visited. "It made a difference for both of us. I started looking forward to seeing him again. I couldn't be more grateful that Scotty showed up that day and taught me what was missing."

When she talks about the experience with other children of aging parents, she often adds, "As hard as it can be to sit in a room with a stark reminder of what aging has done to your parents, you'll never regret whatever effort it took for you to be there. Listening to my father's friends interact with him taught me things about him I didn't know.

"He was a good, good father. But hearing about the men he'd influenced when I thought he was spending his workdays punching a time clock and repairing railway tracks changed my perspective about my father. About the person my father was. What I discovered about him when he was beyond telling me made those visits more significant than I could have imagined."

What are you learning about your aging parents that will become a treasured memory?

I live in a room that isn't my own.
I eat at a table that's foreign to me.
I room with a person I'm not sure I like.
They bring me black coffee; I'd rather have tea.

All that once was familiar is gone.
My earthly treasures, all stored or sold.
My family lives such busy lives,
While I'm supposed to be content to be old.

My days are the same, a hapless routine.
I'd choose to leave, but I have no say.
No control over where I go, what I do.
But you visited me and made my day!

You couldn't stay long, and I understood.
It didn't matter so much how long you could stay.
But you took the time, you went out of your way,
You visited me and made my day.

(Taken from a *Heartbeat of the Home* radio broadcast.)

CHAPTER THIRTY-THREE

When No One Understands or Knows How to Help

*It is one of the most challenging phrases
for the human heart to express:
I need help.*

The only people among us who haven't or won't know the unique season of watching our parents age are those whose parents are uninvolved in their lives or those whose parents die too soon.

The topic of aging parents is more universal than child-raising. Thinking that no one in the world can possibly understand how we feel, what we're experiencing, why we celebrate the microscopic joys as well as the large ones, how tiring it is to care this deeply and feel inadequate to make a difference—despite how we feel, we are not alone.

Those around us have either been there or will be one day. Each family dynamic is different, but few of us escape the reality of aging parents.

And few of us have perfected the art of asking for help when we need it.

But God didn't intend for us to maneuver through this season alone or without help. Just as any parent would be blessed to see his or her children or community coming together for a common cause, God applauds when His children run to each other's aid. When God's people help shoulder the burden of another, the moment vibrates with the divine touch of God's hands.

In the biblical record, think of the friends who cut a hole in the roof of the building where Jesus ministered, then picked up the mat on which the paralyzed man lay in order to let their friend down through the ceiling so he could catch the attention of the Healer.

Think about the father who cared for his emotionally tortured son, a young man so troubled that he screamed out and cut himself with sharp objects and threw himself into a fire every chance he got. Frustrated and concerned, almost out of his own mind, the father cared for and about his tormented son and made sure Jesus knew about it.

Think of Ruth, who cared for her mother-in-law, Naomi, when she was beside herself with grief. Think of the friends who, though misguided in their thinking, attempted to visit and comfort Job.

The stories of the Lord's healing work are interspersed with subplots of the caregiving of humans who acted in His name.

"So be merciful," reads Luke 6:36 (AMPC), "(sympathetic, tender, responsive, and compassionate) even as your Father is [all these]."

Can you imagine how much He is moved when He sees His people rally around those whose parents are aging?

Not so many years ago, the care of aging parents wasn't a question of "Will I?" but "How?" It wasn't unusual for households to contain not only a nuclear family, but extended arms of live-in grandparents and great-grand-parents or elderly aunts or uncles. Caring for the aged and infirm was part of the tapestry of life.

We lost some of the how-to when multigenerational living became less common in American culture. We lost some of the natural rhythm of caring for aging parents and grandparents when living-in became less prevalent. But as our country ages—a higher percentage of elderly in need every year—caregiving needs also increase. Caregiver wisdom and ideas increase.

So does the need for caregivers to know what to say when someone asks, "How can I help?" or when the child of an aging parent musters the courage to say those difficult words—"I need help."

Are you ready with an answer when a friend or family member asks how they can help? Caregiving and aging groups celebrate "random acts of kindness" for those caring for aging parents. Do any of these ideas stir your own imagination—either as an answer for those who want to help you or as tips for how you can help others who are caring for *their* aging parents?

- Offer to make a post office/grocery store/hardware store run for the caregiver.
- Offer to take care of lawn work or snow removal. (My husband mows the lawn of an elderly woman caring for her declining husband. She took such pride in her lawn and mourned that she could no longer do that task herself. But having a

tangible way to ease her load is so rewarding for my husband.)

- Help connect the caregiver to a grocery delivery service.
- Arrange to have small home or appliance repairs taken care of. They often get neglected when an aging parent requires full-time attention.
- Volunteer to put gas in the car or to serve as the taxi service for a doctor's appointment.
- When possible, offer to pick up prescriptions.
- Arrange for a team of trusted people from church to make regular visits to the elderly.
- Give the caregiver a gift certificate for a spa day and arrange respite care for that time (or it won't happen).
- Help with holiday shopping.
- Have flowers sent to the house.
- Offer to walk the dog.
- Volunteer to return library books.
- Arrange for a housekeeper every two weeks, every month, or for spring and fall deep cleaning.
- Save a vacation day to use to provide respite care.
- Deliver a favorite meal.
- Send a handwritten note of encouragement.
- Offer to take the trash from the house to the curb.
- Listen leisurely.

- Keep the household supplied with fresh vegetables and fruit from the farmers' market or your garden.
- Volunteer to handle one of the items on the never-ending to-do list.
- Offer to have a professional photographer take pictures of the aging parent and the caregiving child together.
- Mail the parent or the caregiving child a care package of small gifts or goodies.
- Write out your recent prayers for the caregiver.

You as the child of aging parents are unlikely to hand this list to friends who want to help. Not that it would be a bad idea, since those who long to help often mourn the lack of ideas. But being willing to ask for help and then being willing to give an answer when asked provides a conduit for blessing that flows both ways.

You are not alone. Help is on the way. God may be speaking right now to a friend or family member about you and your needs. Get ready to be blessed.

And the child of aging parents said,
"Help!"

And God answered,
"Okay."

CHAPTER THIRTY-FOUR

When My Efforts Seem So Small

How serious was He when God said,
"If you are faithful in the little things . . ."?

I painted my mother's toenails today," Arla said. "Such a small thing. A few minutes of my time. A few cents' worth of polish. Mom responded as if I'd given her the world. Why do I always assume that what she needs from me is a large display of my love?"

Warren had run out of ideas for connecting with his aging father. His father's interests had paled; his energy level barely registered. Warren sometimes leaned close to make sure his father was still breathing.

"Napping with my eyes open," his dad would say.

"Let's watch your favorite TV show."

"Nah. I've seen all the episodes."

Warren reached for the remote. "But you have a stronger tolerance for reruns than anyone I know, Dad. Let's check out—"

"I said I wasn't interested."

Day after day, the silence between them stretched longer. Then, one day, Warren brought his father a small package.

"What's that?"

"Headphones and an mp3 player, Dad."

"What for?"

"I downloaded a bunch of music I thought you might like."

"Not that head-banging stuff you listen to, is it?"

Warren sighed. "Dad, I'm a worship pastor. It's praise music."

"You know very well what I mean."

The son adjusted the lightweight headphones for his father. "See what you think."

Warren's father listened for a moment. "This is from the forties and fifties."

"I know, Dad."

A tear trickled down the old man's cheek as he said, "Would you turn it up a little?"

Sandie and her mother shared fewer and fewer common interests as her mother's medical condition deteriorated. But they'd always enjoyed watching romantic comedy movies.

"After my mom came to live with me," Sandie said, "one Saturday afternoon we were watching TV together. It was a really terrible 'comedy' movie. Just awful. But in one scene, a hearse slammed on the brakes at a stop sign and the coffin in the back flew out the rear door into the street—and then the hearse drove on without it.

"My mom turned to me and said, 'Now that's what I call a bad day.'

"We had a good laugh about it. So many cares drifted away on that laughter."

Sandie hesitated before telling me, "When I was in the

limo behind the hearse for my mom's funeral, we had to brake suddenly. I was instantly taken back to that moment with my mom, and I started to laugh.

"Pretty soon I was doubled over, much to my brother's horror. I tried to explain, but I was laughing so hard that I couldn't.

"I had to sit in the limo for twenty minutes before I could get out. Everyone thought it was because I was so grief-stricken, which, of course, I was. But I knew my mom would have been laughing with me if she'd been there. God gave me a gift that day—a small but meaningful memory of my mother's sense of humor."

Sometimes as our parents age, we're overwhelmed by unkeepable promises, seemingly unmendable fences, and concerns for their unspeakable pain. We're weighed down by untenable problems, forced to make uncomfortable decisions, troubled by unanswered—or so we think— prayers.

But in the middle of all of it, our spirits are lifted by unquenchable hope, unfathomable peace, unending joy that is promised to us from a God of limitless understanding.

"Great is our Lord and mighty in power; his understanding has no limit," Psalm 147:5 (NIV).

"How great is our Lord! His power is absolute! His understanding is beyond comprehension!" (NLT).

"Great is our Lord, and of great power: his understanding is infinite" (KJV).

We're encouraged, too, by the smallest grace. The hummingbirds outside our parents' window. The softness of our mother's hands. Our father's almost indistinguishable but ocean-deep voice when he prays. The kindness of the medical staff. A cold drink. A warm blanket. A child's hug.

Training ourselves to watch for the small graces that our parents might find uplifting can be an adventure. Graces don't always hide out in the open. And our parents' definitions of a joy-producer may change over time from a gourmet meal to a fresh pillowcase, from a steady stream of music to solid blocks of silence, from a large bouquet of flower-shop flowers to a single stem of Queen Anne's lace.

Judy said, "In 1988 when I was dealing with severe health issues, I had to move home with my parents at the age of thirty-eight. My dad made me his project for the year— determined I would be able to return to work. One of his challenges was for me to walk with him to the end of the block. Oh, how we celebrated when I finally achieved this goal!

"Fast forward all these years. My dad had a stroke and suffers from dementia. When I go back home for a visit, we walk that same block. This time I'm the one encouraging him to reach the corner. Each time we walk our block, I thank the Lord for how He's brought us full circle and that I have the opportunity to give back to my dad in a small, yet meaningful way."

My sisters and I used to sing in an inspirational trio for women's events and mother/daughter banquets. Mom and Dad good-naturedly fought over which one of them was the most supportive. When all three of us were together in Mom's room during her final months on earth, she'd often ask for us to sing to her. We were more than happy to comply. Such a small thing.

We'd sing all her favorite hymns and praise songs, until we'd grown hoarse or had accumulated too large of a crowd in the hall outside Mom's door in the hospice facility, the staff among them.

On what we eventually knew was her final weekend, we swabbed her dry lips and cooled her fevered forehead and held her hands. From time to time, we'd break into song—something fitting for the atmosphere that already had begun to feel celestial.

Mom could answer with one-word whispers when we talked to her, then slip into a sleeplike state for a few minutes or a few hours.

When she seemed especially restless at one point, one of us asked if she wanted us to sing another song.

"No," she whispered. And then a longer stretch of words. "I have to do this myself."

She and Jesus were apparently still in conversation about whether or not she could finally go Home.

The small gift we gave her then was silence. Sitting in her presence, assuring her that we were there, but allowing her the dignity of making her own decision about how she would spend her final moments. Lord, may we always be "faithful in the little things" (Luke 16:10 NLT).

"I need a rocket-launcher, Lord,
Against this vile Goliath."
And God gave David five small stones.

"I need a larger army
Than the thirty thousand, Lord,
To defeat this enemy."
And God gave Gideon three hundred.

"I need a way to ease my parents' pain, Lord."
And God gave
A photograph,
A bottle of fingernail polish,
A song,
A handful of fresh-picked blueberries,
A sun-dried pillowcase.

And God saw that it was good.

CHAPTER THIRTY-FIVE

When the End Is Too Near

*Caring for aging parents
is part of our own maturing process.*

The hardest thing about watching my mother age (now that I'm almost sixty and she's almost eighty)," Candice says, "is knowing that time is passing very quickly. It's the realization of her mortality. And it's also the inevitability of a good-bye that used to seem so far in the distance but is now *foreseeable*."

Teen parents learn quickly that they're not the center of the universe anymore. If they don't learn the lesson, their parenting falls apart. As our parents age, we go through a similar transition, realizing that whether or not we anticipated how all-consuming this season would be, we must either grow up and step up or check out. And checking out was never God's intention.

"All the treasures of wisdom and knowledge are hidden in him" (Colossians 2:3 CEB).

If we try to navigate these rough waters by our instincts alone, we will likely miss the hazards, the warnings that the bridge is out over that stretch of water, the depth-finders, the Class V rapids, the. . . .

God never intended us to bear it all on our shoulders, even though it feels as if that's what's happening sometimes. He offers wisdom. It's hidden in Christ. Hidden, but accessible to those who are looking for it, who remain observant, who spend more time listening for His direction than they do plotting survival techniques.

It is planned obsolescence for the human body to fade and leave the earth—but planned by the heart of a caring, loving God. When autumn arrives in the upper Midwest, colors change and the landscape reveals the "bones" hidden during summer's lush greenery. The woodlands open up visually, with the undergrowth now gone until spring. Winter's on the horizon, its crisp tang in the wind a constant reminder.

Autumn is no accident. It's a carefully orchestrated dance. It's creation's crescendo before its hibernation. Its beauty is the stuff of photo and art galleries. It's a time of harvest and bounty and preparation for the chill of winter and the barren ground that produces nothing.

For a time.

Human life mimics that cycle. The spring of life is pregnant with promise. Growth and soft rains, fragrant breezes, the labor of planting. The lawn sprouts a green more lime than shamrock, then explodes overnight with freckles of dandelions and wood violets. Each day brings a new blossom, new pollen, signs of youth and vigor. Nothing dies but winter's memory.

Summer. Life in full bloom. Color and wildlife and sun in a wild tangle of overgrowth. Strawberries that stain our fingers. Blueberries so warm from the bush that they melt on the tongue. Nectarines. Peaches. Dinner pulled from the garden, peas right out of the pod. Backyard cookouts and campfires with no purpose other than family staring into the same screenless flames.

Autumn. Abundant autumn.

And winter. Life retreats underground. And one step outside—into air that freezes in our lungs—reminds us how vulnerable and mortal we are.

The spirit was built for eternity; the body, for this earth only. This brief season.

"The end of caregiving isn't freedom. It's grief," said Margaret Renkl, in a *New York Times* article called "Caregiving: A Burden So Heavy until It's Gone".

No matter how strong we are through the process of our parents' aging, the day inevitably comes when we realize anew that the dreaded end point is drawing nearer, nearer. Those of solid faith in the mercies of God and the promise of heaven welcome their parents' release from the pain and distresses, the "surly bonds of earth," as John Magee Jr. expressed it in his poem "High Flight."

We sense a shift in our souls, a shift in our caregiving. No longer are we striving to prolong. We're emotionally plumping the pillows in heaven's waiting room, preparing for our parents' arrival. We're readying our hearts and the rest of the family. And we're doubling down in our efforts to make the most of our parents' final days.

For some, those days are a gentle drifting toward the end. For others, it's an agonizing crawl through a tunnel of painful barbed wire.

We are, as the apostle Paul says, torn between the two worlds, uncertain which is better—to be absent from the body and present with the Lord or for our loved one to remain for a while longer among family and friends here on earth (Philippians 1:23–24).

Our family had stayed so long in that "any day now" mode. Mother had outlived all but one of the residents who had come into the hospice center while she was there. Most left within a day or two, not under their own power. When the hospice staff informed us that all signs pointed to the probability that Mom was within two or three days of the end of her journey, life—even the air itself—took on what we can only describe as a holy hush. Her children gathered from various corners of the state. We took turns sitting vigil with brief breaks for tears or sustenance. It had all come to these last few days, these few hours that remained.

Another friend, Davalynn, said that when she walked into her mother's room at the care center one day, her mother greeted her with, "I saw Jesus today."

"I wasn't surprised by her remark," Davalynn said. "Lately she had been seeing things no one else saw.

"'Really, Mom? What was He doing?'

"She pointed to the corner by the door. 'He was right over there. He had dirt on His knees from working in the yard.'

"Not a typically 'holy' vision of the Savior, but more of a down-to-earth visitation. And why not? He was the Creator. She didn't have much more to say about His visit that day, but at least she recognized Him. I took comfort in the fact that she still knew Him, even if she didn't always know me."

As our parents advance in age and their winter nears, we can view that time as the end or as a season for the body, a launchpad for the spirit.

And in those hours, as we have in the months or years leading to that moment, we care for the body and nurture the spirit.

How do I describe
The depth
Of this peace?
Who but You, Lord,
Could prepare a heart
For a moment like this
When the veil between earth
And heaven
Is transparently thin?

CHAPTER THIRTY-SIX

When I'm Already Grieving

More people than we know
who care for aging parents
have a head start on grieving
long before the end.

Carolyn said, "My sister and I watched my mom grow so dependent upon us. Always proud to do things on her own, she was heartbroken, and so were we.

"Mom had struggled all her life for something better for her children. We were a product of divorce. Mom fought a hard battle with her health until one day she said, 'I can't do this anymore.' I knew then that I was going to lose my best friend. But I'd started missing her long before that moment."

"My dad died two years ago," Lorna said. "His mind was sharp until the end. One of the last times I picked him up from the hospital, he said, 'Where are the hubcaps on your car?'

"I told him, 'They came off, one by one. I haven't had time to get new ones.'

"He said, 'It's bad for my image to ride around in a car without hubcaps. We're going to go get you some right now.'

"So instead to taking him home from the hospital, I drove him to the auto-parts store, where he insisted on going in with me to pick them out and buy them. He might have been dying, but he still wanted to take care of his little girl.

"That," Lorna said, "was the kind of dad he was and the reason why my grief process started early."

Karen tells of an important healing layer in her grieving

process. "Last Christmas, my husband received a gift of a machine that converts VHS tapes to DVDs. He pulled out some old VHS tapes and began the process.

"One of those tapes was his parents' fiftieth wedding anniversary. We watched it and then the camera showed the door—and in walked my mother. We figured out she was sixty-five at the time. She was so beautiful and happy. She went around the room charming everyone she met.

"It was an amazing moment for me because I'd been filled with such guilt and pain over her final months on earth, and all I'd been able to think about was how she was in the end—ornery and scarred, scared and out of her mind.

"I had forgotten," Karen said, "what an absolutely wonderful, charming, and beautiful person she was and what a great mother she had been to me before she began to fail.

"I am so grateful to God for those moments recorded on tape. They helped put my grief in a new light. Oh, that God would grant me a sharp memory of the years before, when she was healthy and happy and fun."

If we have prior warning about a parent's imminent death it's natural that we begin the grieving process early. And it's not unhealthy if that knowledge presses us into God's embrace and helps us fully embrace the dying parent.

How do we manage our emotions when we know the end is drawing near?

Some find ways to commemorate the life and legacy of

their beloved parent by choosing an item that represents who the parent was before the negative effects of aging faded the picture.

I have recipe cards in my mom's penmanship—stained with fingerprints and butter. Those cards are a treasure.

I have examples of my father's penmanship too. Distinctive, almost architectural. And his handwritten sermon notes from the 1950s. I also have a cherished recording of his final band concert, which was just two months before his sudden death.

When we siblings divided the contents of Mom's apartment before her death (she insisted—she wanted that all taken care of before she breathed her last), we each chose one item that meant something to us. One brother took our father's triangle-folded flag from his service in the Marines. Another sibling took some of the many books Mom had collected. We each found something that resonated with us. I took a small ceramic pitcher that Mom had used years ago in pouring water over our little-girl heads to rinse out ammonia-heavy perm solutions.

A good friend of mine makes memorial jewelry from fingerprints—pendants, rings, and pins. She mails a kit to a family member. Inside the kit is a mold and polymer for making an impression of a loved one's fingerprint— even down to a tiny baby's. Then my artist friend creates gallery-quality jewelry pieces with the impression embedded in sterling silver, surrounded by semiprecious or precious stones. I wish I'd known about her artwork while my parents were still alive.

Amanda's memory is imprinted on her heart rather than in sterling silver. "I remember my grandfather deteriorating over a six-month period from cancer. My mother and I took care of him as he got worse. One of the last events he was able to attend was at a supper club. I remember walking up to him and giving him a hug. He melted into me. As much as I knew he loved me, he didn't ever show affection. That moment is a memory I will have forever."

When grief has gotten a toehold in us, it's more than time to start collecting the memories and tender moments that will cushion grief's blows. Those whose parents deal with dementia or Alzheimer's often report that their grieving process starts at the beginning of the disease and spreads out over the entire journey. Their grief seems almost spent by the time the end comes.

And then they discover a new version of grieving.

As each aging parent is an individual, so are our individual methods, lengths, and styles of grieving. But no matter how individual in nature, one anchor point secures us—our hope in Christ.

You are my hope, Lord. You, Lord,
are the one I've trusted since childhood.
I've depended on you from birth—
You cut the cord when I came
from my mother's womb.
My praise is always about you.

—Psalm 71:5–6 CEB

From the end of the earth will I cry unto thee,
when my heart is overwhelmed:
lead me to the rock that is higher than I.

—Psalm 61:2 KJV

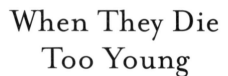

CHAPTER THIRTY-SEVEN

When They Die Too Young

To die when age has swallowed all joy,
To die before age has had a chance to mature;
We can survive neither without the Giver of Life.

The father of former NFL quarterback and Heisman–Trophy winner Doug Flutie died of a heart attack while in the hospital for an unrelated illness. The news rocked Flutie and his family. They'd barely taken in that news when, within an hour, his mother died of a sudden heart attack as well. Flutie lost both parents within a few minutes of each other. In interviews, Flutie said, "They say you can die of a broken heart, and I believe it."

With our attention in these pages on those whose parents are aging, our sensitivity increases for those whose parents died too young.

As I mentioned earlier, my dad didn't have the opportunity to age. He stepped into heaven before he could step into retirement, Social Security, or the number that once denoted "old." At sixty-four, his heart failed him.

My father and mother had devoted themselves wholeheartedly to their chosen professions. Mom had retired early from nursing. Dad had little desire to retire, but he and Mom planned that when he reached sixty-five, he would lay down his director's baton and they would travel across the United States in an RV, stopping at national parks and reconnecting with friends they'd made over the years.

In going through some of my mother's papers just a few years ago, I discovered a note about one of the most poignant moments following Dad's death. The two of them had already ordered an RV. Mom had to call and cancel the order.

Sheila says that her greatest grief is not having had the opportunity to be there for her parents as they aged. "Both of my parents died of sudden illnesses. They were laughing one day and gone in an instant. Mom, at a vibrant sixty-nine, broke her leg and died of what the doctors suspected later was a blood clot. Daddy died almost a year later of a heart attack. He, too, was active and still ran his farm."

Some claim that any time a parent dies, it's too soon.

Those who watch a parent linger through a long, draining illness or in a state that dangles precariously between this life and the next—or those who sit in a vigil over a parent whose dying process is a belly-crawl through a minefield of excruciating pain might disagree. *Would* disagree.

Psalm 6:3 (NIV) reads, "My soul is in deep anguish. How long, Lord, how long?" It's a cry heard over many a deathbed. From the lips of the dying. From the lips of those encircling the bed.

But other cries reach God's ears.

"I didn't have a chance to say good-bye."

"I was still in the air, on my way to his side, when he breathed his last. So many regrets."

"Our last conversation by phone ended poorly. I was irritable and tired. My mother knew how to bring that out of me. But it's not how I wanted our relationship to end. If I'd known we'd never share another conversation. . . ."

"I promised myself—and my kids—that I'd cut through all the passive-aggressive dance moves my father and I knew and finally tell him how I really felt. I wanted us to start fresh. We didn't have the chance."

"What I most regret is that I didn't tell her I loved her."

"What I most regret is that I never heard my father tell me he loved me."

Too soon. Too soon.

And we're asked to believe—by faith—that long before we're born, God is aware of the length of our days, the span of our parents' lives. The same God who orders our steps, who knows the end from the beginning—and our end—is the One who provides for the ache of unfulfilled longings and soul-piercing regrets.

My maternal grandmother died when my mother was starting her sixth year as a parent, with her fourth child a newborn. Mom often talked about how much she missed not having her mother to consult as she raised her children. Mom was competent and accomplished, a strong woman with strong opinions and exceptional nursing skills. But she felt the absence of the woman who for nine months had felt my mom's heart beat under hers. The woman who taught her to stand. To read. To draw the lines that spelled "Dorothy." The mother who shook her head when her daughter skipped away from supper cleanup to ride her horse or who opted to help her brothers bale hay rather than learn to bake bread. The mother who scolded her and loved her and could have taught her how to manage life's harsh seasons.

My grandmother had survived the loss of a child to cancer. She'd fed her family during reed-thin lean years. She'd welcomed a troubled brother-in-law into her home, endured his debilitating depression, and quietly cleaned up the mess after he shot himself in their living room.

When my mom was barely alive in those last few days, she said I had Grandma Stone's laugh. I didn't know my grandmother well enough or long enough to have heard her laugh. But I wish I'd let Mom hear it more often.

Within the last week, two acquaintances told me that they were teens when a parent died. *Too soon. Too soon.* They never had the opportunity to experience the parent-child relationship as adult-to-adult. They missed having the parent proud and present for high-school graduation, college graduation, wedding, first grandchild, first gray hair.

And now they are approaching aging with no family precedence as a landmark.

The camaraderie of loss links those whose parents die too soon and those who live to whatever the current definition is of "ripe old age." Loss binds us together. Sympathy flows both ways. Compassion for one another's pain builds community. If we let it.

"Bear one another's burdens," the apostle Paul tells us in Galatians 6:2 (ESV). That's God's heart—that we help shoulder each other's burdens as our parents age . . . or when they aren't given the opportunity to age.

Who do you know is grieving a parent who died too soon? Is it you? A friend? A young person in your church? A neighbor? How can you—even in a small, but hope-giving way—help shoulder that person's heartache, identify with their struggle, or meet a practical need?

God designed it so the weight we bear, crushing as it seems, grows lighter when we offer to help carry the weight that stoops another. It defies explanation, but it's true.

The common thread
Woven through
Humanity
Unbreakable
Inescapable
Unavoidable
With no regard
For status
Or ethnicity
For race
Or education
For accomplishment
Or lack of it
For gender
Or politics
Or age
Is grief.
Grief unites us.
Makes us one.

We have that in common.

CHAPTER THIRTY-EIGHT

When My Skills and Love Are No Longer Enough

Don't let the best you have done so far
be the standard for the rest of your life.
—GUSTAVUS F. SWIFT

For me to not be able to lift my mother's spirits is just one of the most disheartening things that I've ever had to endure," Marcus said.

Xochitl says, "During our months at the cancer-care center, I slept in a rented recliner. While serving as my mom's live-in caregiver, I struggled with my own recovery from multiple surgeries and injections in my shoulders and upper thoracic back.

"I still ache when I remember the night my mom's soft voice hung in the darkness that separated us as we prepared to sleep on opposite ends of the room.

"'You can lie down with me, if you want,' she said.

"I declined. 'I don't want to disturb your sleep if I move too much.'

"Now, I recognize her invitation as a plea for closeness. Thinking back, I can identify lots of times I missed her hidden requests for comfort. We wore shields of faith and brave warrior masks as we navigated around personal loneliness and heartache.

"I excelled at hiding emotions, wanting to be strong for her, needing to hold myself together for her, when all I wanted to do was fall into my mom's arms and sob.

"Although Mom affirmed how much she appreciated all I'd done, I've often wished I had been more selfish. I wish I would have hugged her, even when she acted strong. I wish I would have had the courage to acknowledge that my faith was still strong, even though I needed to break down and cry, voice my frustrations, and share my fears and insecurities.

"If I had been brave enough to admit my struggles with feeling weak, scared, and overwhelmed at times, maybe my mom would have felt safe enough to say, 'Me too!'

"Maybe the pain would have been easier to bear if we'd both had the guts to be vulnerable and assure each other that we were in this hard journey together."

What qualifies us for serving either our aging parents or Christ is not perfection, unparalleled talent, finely honed skill, or even a sound body. What is required above all else is a willing heart. There are no hardship deferments.

Bill G. says, "God is father to the fatherless, He'll step in to fill gaps we can't. He loves our parents more than we do, and He'll love them when we can't. We're not in this alone; omnipotent love is on our side."

The day comes to many children of aging parents when it's obvious that our efforts are no longer enough. Our own health is deteriorating, or theirs is. They need the kind of pain management that's not possible at home. Their physical care is beyond our limitations. Their mental or emotional state is a threat to others living in the home. Or, our parents make the hard call.

My mother's desire was not to live with her children. She wanted to spare us the rigors of full-time caregiving.

Plus, I'm pretty sure each of our busy schedules would have tried her patience to the breaking point. It was her decision to have in-home hospice care at her apartment for as long as possible. We served her in every way we could, but she preferred that some of the care we would have done was accomplished by hospice workers so when we visited, we could talk. Her choice. We complied.

The day came when she called those of us who lived closest and asked for a mini family meeting. Breathless and pale, she said, "I don't think I can do this anymore. What do you think about calling the House of the Dove and seeing if they have a room for me?"

I can still feel the tears that pooled. She'd done things her way. She'd endured more than most humans could, but she knew she'd reached the end of her resources and stamina. Yet she consulted with us. She wanted to know we approved. We did.

She thought she'd held out until the second of August by sheer determination. Because she planned everything carefully, she expected to die by August third so the funeral could be over and done with before the start of the new school year.

That was my mom.

But once safely tucked into the hospice residence, she rallied a little. Then a little more. The actual date of her homegoing was February fifteenth. She'd gotten another of her wishes. My grandfather was buried on my birthday. My father was buried on my birthday. She wanted to be buried on my birthday.

In August, that seemed a dream she'd have to surrender.

In November, we tried to console her that Christmas would go on without her.

In mid-February, we visited the funeral home the day after her death and realized that she would indeed be buried on my birthday.

For some, the moment when our skills and love are no longer enough comes far earlier in the process, when a memory-care facility or nursing home or assisted living is the best option. That decision has never been an easy one in all the history of parents and homes for the elderly.

"He may not notice," Glenn said, "but we'll choose a place for Dad with a great garden because of how much he loved his flowers. We'll choose a place where he can have his own chair, his own pictures, because we know how much that would mean to him. We'll choose a place close enough to home that the few friends who are brave enough to visit him can still do that. And when he hollers and screams and throws a tantrum? We'll have to ignore the noise and pray he'll settle in eventually. Who's to say he wouldn't be belligerent and angry if he were able to stay at home?"

Julie's father's care had become far more than she

could physically manage. The family knew it was time. But he insisted he could care for himself. That hadn't been true for years. And he fought the decision like a cornered bull, until three weeks into his stay. His resentment dissipated. He made friends and found peace. His relationship with Julie and his other children settled into a far less stressful season with confidence that his physical needs were getting the attention they deserved.

The family could then focus attention on who their father was as a person, on rehearsing cherished memories and creating new ones.

No one can make those housing decisions or end-of-life-care decisions alone or without wise counsel.

But God speaks to a listening heart. And one of His messages during those "I can't do this anymore" days is "[I know. I'm here.] My power is made perfect in your weakness" (see 2 Corinthians 12:9 NIV).

A place with a garden
A river
A view
A place with the things
That matter to you

A friend in the next room
And one down the hall
Staff members kind
Who respond when you call

This is my prayer
When the time comes to leave
This place you call home
Because you matter to me.

CHAPTER THIRTY-NINE

When the Moment Comes to Say Good-bye

When someone you love becomes a memory,

the memory becomes a treasure.

—AUTHOR UNKNOWN

On hearing the news of her terminal illness, author and lecturer Phyllis Tickle said, "The dying is my next career."

"Scott and I were newlyweds," Jody said. "I vividly remember a Sunday afternoon when we received an alarming phone call from his mother asking us to hurry over to the local hospital. Scott's grandfather Carl had been admitted there the week before. His heart condition had taken a quick turn for the worse.

"We gathered our belongings and rushed over as quickly as we could. When we arrived at Carl's hospital room, we found Scott's mom and grandmother Elsie pacing nervously around his beside, looking helpless and forlorn.

"We gave them each a hug around their tears. Grandpa Carl lay there looking lifeless. His eyes were closed. All we could hear was his labored breathing.

"Words failed us and seemed all too awkward at such a fragile time, so we sat in somber silence.

"After some time passed," Jody said, "I felt a nudge in my spirit. My mind became flooded with a serenade of beautiful hymns and choruses. I motioned to Scott to lean closer to me, and I whispered an idea that came to mind. He smiled and nodded in agreement.

"We both got up and walked over to where Grandpa

Carl was lying and quietly knelt beside his bed, gently taking hold of each of his warm, frail hands. We began singing familiar hymns and choruses, one after the other, with tears streaming down our faces.

"Though Grandpa Carl's eyes remained closed, a gentle smile seemed to grace his face, and all of a sudden he began squeezing our hands as if trying to communicate, 'Please don't stop. Please keep singing.'

"Peace and serenity seemed to blanket the room. Scott's mom and grandma looked calm, no longer pacing, no longer sobbing. The music ministered comfort to their grieving spirits."

Love. Music. Family. God's Word. Memories. Sweet tears. Prayer. Voices. Comfort. Final words. The decor of a room about to witness the thin veil between heaven and earth melting away.

Discussion, argument, self-absorption, analysis, planning, debate—they're for a different time and place. Except for the self-absorption and argument portions. They have no place when it comes to walking an aging parent Home.

"Take courage, Mom. You're almost there."

"I only have to hang on to my courage until God calls me home."

Cherie remembers when it came time to say good-bye to her grandfather. "He had been diagnosed with bone cancer and was under hospice care.

"I got there late after putting in a full day at work. He wasn't in the mood to talk since he'd had visitors all day. I said that was fine with me. Instead I held his hand, and we sat quietly that way for a long time before he finally went to sleep.

"It was the last time I talked to him. The next day he was in a catatonic state. Unfortunately, someone he didn't like all that well was by his bedside, touching his arm.

"I worried that he would die while this person had their hands on him, and I didn't want him to go to glory feeling annoyed. (Isn't that a silly thing to think?) So I protectively put my arms around him and held him.

"I told him how wonderful he was to me, how the only thing that brought me comfort right then was knowing he would be there for us on the other side and that it would be all be okay. A tear formed on the side of his eye. I wiped it away, and within moments he was gone. He died in my arms.

"It was a gift from above, that moment," Cherie said. "I felt such blessings in being able to say good-bye to my grandfather in such a peaceful and loving way."

Debbie's experience was similarly sweet. "Mom, during her dying time, lay nearly unresponsive in her nursing-home bed. But she grabbed hold of the hymnal I was singing from and held it close to her. When I began to sing 'Be Thou My Vision,' her eyes remained closed, but she fumbled for the hymnal and sang the first two verses, still with her eyes closed.

"And then she became unresponsive again," Debbie said. "She sang many years in the church choir. Spending her final lucid moments this way seemed so appropriate."

"My mom had early-onset Alzheimer's," Diane said, "and lived about the last ten years of her life in a mostly noncommunicative state. But she would walk the halls of the nursing home and sing hymns.

"She lived much longer than most after diagnosis, but when the end was near, her children and grandchildren gathered at her bedside. I sat on her bed, holding her hand as she struggled to breathe. Having no doubt about her eternal destiny, I whispered, 'Mom, it's okay. You can go home now. We all love you.'

"She smiled, took one final breath, and was gone. I will never forget that smile."

Helen's mom prayed with her less than twenty-four hours before her homegoing at age ninety-seven. Her mother prayed, "Lord, bless [each immediate family member by name] and take them all to heaven someday. And, Jesus, I love You, but why are You taking so long?"

Jennifer's father-in-law was completely deaf. In the moments before his final breaths, he signed to his wife, who was also deaf, "I hear music." What a tender gift from the heart of God.

May will always treasure a moment with her grandmother that affirms how close Jesus hovers when the end is near. "My grandma had Alzheimer's. The last time I was able to get leave from the army, we went to Wisconsin and visited her. She just put her hand on my stomach and gave me her sweet smile without saying anything. We hadn't told anyone yet, but we were expecting. She sensed it. God must have allowed her that insight as a joy-gift just for her. And us."

Wanda says, "Before I had any connection with Jesus, my mother was diagnosed with cancer. She called me at work to give me the outcome of her last surgery and begged me to come right away to the hospital.

"I could not go alone. I called her mom and we went together. Telling my grandma that her daughter was dying, terminal, with weeks to live, was horrible. I had no hope, no Jesus. But Grandma did.

"In those last months, Grandma and I lived with my mom and her husband—my stepfather—caring for her. The night Mom died, my grandmother rose to her feet as Mom breathed her last and said 'Praise the Lord!' I ran from the room. I had no idea who this God was, but Grandma did. Within months of my mother's death, my grandmother made sure I knew."

What are the common denominators in these stirring "time to say good-bye" stories from those who've completed the journey with their aging parents? Rock-ribbed, hope-hemmed faith in God.

The Strength-Giver, Song-Writer, Idea-Creator, Love-Generator, and Sustainer God.

"Precious in the sight of the LORD is the death of his faithful servants" (Psalm 116:15 NIV).

It wasn't until I stood there
At the end of it all
That process I thought I couldn't survive

It wasn't until I knew my work was done
That I believed I could actually do it

It wasn't until then, Lord,
Wrapped in Your love
As a comfort for my loss
That I knew, really knew
You would be
All I needed.

CHAPTER FORTY

When I Shift to Life without My Parents

And when their voices are stilled,
another is heard in the mist—
the cry of the newly orphaned.

N. L. B. Horton penned this stirring, heart-gripping story.

"I'll receive Dad's ashes tomorrow. They mark the end of a wild and horrific elder-care adventure that started eight months ago. Responsibilities as executor will continue for at least nine months. I hope to breathe again when I celebrate Christ's resurrection next Easter.

"Dad's ashes will bookend Mother's, which sit in a box on a shelf in my office—to the right of A. A. Milne books from my childhood, above books on feminist theology. Mother died a week before Christmas.

"Where I live, winter hits hard. Scattering her ashes across the snowfield would have left a grey streak that screamed, "Mother is dead!" for months. She would have returned to haunt me for leaving her out there like that, even though I'm confident that she has better things to do in heaven—such as glorify God and love Him forever.

"So I waited for spring. When our meadow is rich with asters and wild roses, populated with deer and elk, foxes, and the occasional bear and mountain lion all summer. Below the subalpine grassland where the Patagonian shepherds herd masses of sheep each June and the fireworks burst above the spruce forest on the Fourth of July.

"Then Dad's health failed. Scattering them together would be a fitting tribute to an almost sixty-seven-year marriage, and I braced for impact.

"Flights back and forth became more frequent. Decisions became more complex. Do I authorize a biopsy if the surgeons can't treat what they think they'll find? Does he need to move from assisted living to a nursing home? Do we *really* have to discuss hospice-level care? How do I weigh sanctity of life against terminal illness?

"I am confident about eternity, believing what I learned while studying for my master's degree from a fine seminary. I 'get' heaven. But reaching eternity was proving difficult for the second time in four months. I kept praying.

"I had just returned from keeping Dad calm during a collapsed lung when I got the call. His health had taken a dramatic turn for the worse. We were in the middle of a bodacious spring snowstorm. The pass between the airport and me was closed, so I received updates every hour or two for forty-eight hours.

"Before the storm ended, he died. As my father's daughter, I reel from the loss.

"I'll receive Dad's ashes tomorrow. When I celebrate Christ's resurrection next Easter, I'll also look forward to the Second Coming. With my parents, I will glorify God and love Him forever. Hallelujah."

With my father long gone, my mother's death in 2010 made me an orphan. Before I left the hospice residence, before the coroner arrived, I already felt like an orphan. Many others have expressed a similar sensation. No matter how old we are, when our last remaining parent passes, something within us cries out like the parentless child we have become.

We go on. We all do. But not without a significant shift in our approach to life and faith and forever.

Mary Elizabeth says, "One of the things I wasn't prepared for was 'the after' when my Mom died. Caring for both my mother-in-law and my own mother for a period of nine and a half years changed me and put my life on hold. I wouldn't do it differently, but maybe I'd learn to plan a little better for the inevitable day when they were no longer the center of it.

"I also didn't take care of myself the way I should have," Mary Elizabeth added, "thinking there just wasn't enough time.

"Long-term illness of a loved one takes a lot out of a person. I am still working through the repercussions almost two years later. God held me together through the process and was my greatest source of help. My husband and son shared the journey with me. Isolation is part of it during that time. Following the loss, one needs to venture out and make new relationships. And that can be hard."

Valeri said, "We didn't expect Mom to live long after the surgery that removed part of her brain, but again, she fooled us. Twenty years or so later, I realized that I had put my life on hold, waiting for her passing."

So, we learn to live through it? That's the lesson?

No.

Through it—through caring well for our aging parents, through watching God meet their every need and ours, through having all the fluff trimmed away because it doesn't fit and never did satisfy, through walking our parent Home— through all of that, we learn to live.

My prayer for you, reader:
May you be "strengthened through his glorious might
so that you endure everything
and have patience . . .
giving thanks with joy to the Father.

COLOSSIANS 1:11–12 CEB

Jesus's words to you:
"Your care for others is the measure of your greatness."

LUKE 9:48 TLB

Other Books by Cynthia Ruchti

(NonFiction)

Tattered and Mended: The Art of Healing the Wounded Soul
Ragged Hope: Surviving the Fallout of Other People's Choices

(Fiction)

Restoring Christmas
A Fragile Hope
Song of Silence
An Endless Christmas
As Waters Gone By
All My Belongings
When the Morning Glory Blooms
They Almost Always Come Home

Contributing Author

(Devotionals and Journals)

Be Still and Let Your Nail Polish Dry: 365-Day Devotional Journal
Grace Is Like Chocolate without the Calories
Mornings with Jesus 2017
Mornings with Jesus 2016
Mornings with Jesus 2015
Mornings with Jesus 2014
His Grace Is Sufficient . . . Decaf Is Not
A Joyful Heart
A Cup of Comfort for Writers

ABOUT THE AUTHOR

Cynthia Ruchti tells stories hemmed in hope. She's the award-winning author of more than twenty books and a frequent speaker for women's ministry events. She serves as the professional relations liaison for American Christian Fiction Writers, helping retailers, libraries, and book clubs discover good books and connect with authors. She lives with her husband in Central Wisconsin.

Visit Cynthia at www.cynthiaruchti.com

IF YOU ENJOYED THIS BOOK, WILL YOU CONSIDER SHARING THE MESSAGE WITH OTHERS?

Mention the book in a blog post or through Facebook, Twitter, Pinterest, or upload a picture through Instagram.

Recommend this book to those in your small group, book club, workplace, and classes.

Head over to facebook.com/CynthiaRuchtiReaderPage, "LIKE" the page, and post a comment as to what you enjoyed the most.

Tweet "I recommend reading #AsMyParentsAge by @cynthiaruchti // @worthypub"

Pick up a copy for someone you know who would be challenged and encouraged by this message.

Write a book review online.

Visit us at **worthypublishing.com**

twitter.com/worthypub

worthypub.tumblr.com

facebook.com/worthypublishing

pinterest.com/worthypub

instagram.com/worthypub

youtube.com/worthypublishing